MEDICAL TECHNOLOGY:
INVENTING
THE
INSTRUMENTS

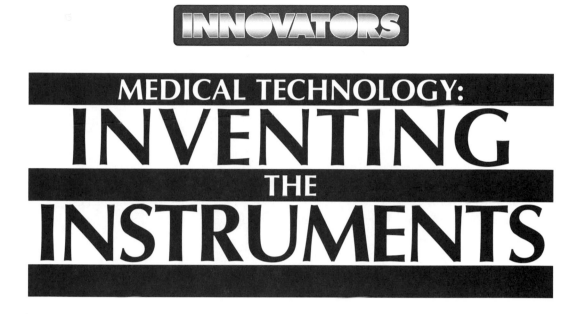

INNOVATORS

MEDICAL TECHNOLOGY:
INVENTING
THE
INSTRUMENTS

Robert Mulcahy

The Oliver Press, Inc.
Minneapolis

The Oliver Press, Inc.
Charlotte Square
5707 West 36th Street
Minneapolis, MN 55416-2510

Library of Congress Cataloging-in-Publication Data
Mulcahy, Robert, 1971-
Medical technology: inventing the instruments / Robert Mulcahy.
p.   cm.—(Innovators)
Includes bibliographical references and index.
   Summary: Profiles the life and work of seven scientists who
made important medical inventions, including Santorio and
the thermometer, Laënnec and the stethoscope, and Roentgen
and the X ray.
ISBN 1-881508-34-X (library binding)
1. Medical scientists—Biography—Juvenile literature.
2. Biologists—Biography—Juvenile literature. 3. Medical
instruments and apparatus—Juvenile literature. [1. Medical
instruments and apparatus—History. 2. Scientists.
3. Inventions.]
I. Title. II. Series.
R134.M854
610' .28'092—dc20
[B]   96-4939
                                        CIP
                                        AC
ISBN 1-881508-34-X
Innovators III
Printed in the United States of America

03 02 01 00 99 98 97   8 7 6 5 4 3 2 1

CONTENTS

Medicine in the Seventeenth Century

In the 1600s, a remarkable period in the history of Europe was ending. The Renaissance had been a time of great discoveries and a transition between the medieval (approximately A.D. 500-1400) and modern eras. (The word renaissance means rebirth or revival.) This awakening in all endeavors—religious, political, artistic, and scientific, including medicine— had begun in the 1300s in Italy and then spread to the rest of the continent by the following century. Famous innovators of this time included Leonardo da Vinci, who used his artistic skill and engineering genius to design buildings and many devices, such as the first elevator, which was installed in a Milan cathedral. Michelangelo (1475-1564) influenced the art world with his beautiful sculptures and murals. Galileo Galilei (1564-1642), astronomer and physicist, tested theories of gravity and velocity and proved that the earth and other planets circle the sun—still a revolutionary idea at the time.

Leonardo da Vinci (1452-1519) was one of the leading figures of the Renaissance.

Beginning during the Renaissance, modern medicine emerged gradually. The practice of medicine in Europe during the 1600s was still based on some very old ideas. More than 2,000 years earlier, the ancient Greeks taught that the human body was a balance of four humors: blood, yellow bile, black bile, and phlegm. Each humor originated in a specific body organ and was associated with two of four fundamental qualities—hot, dry, wet, and cold—and one of the four elements—air, fire, earth, and water.

The blending of these humors in each person resulted in a "temperament." There were four main temperaments: sanguine (hot and moist), phlegmatic (cold and moist), choleric (hot and dry), and melancholic (cold and dry). If the humors were out

The theory that human health depended on the balance of humors, illustrated here, influenced medical practices for more than 2,000 years.

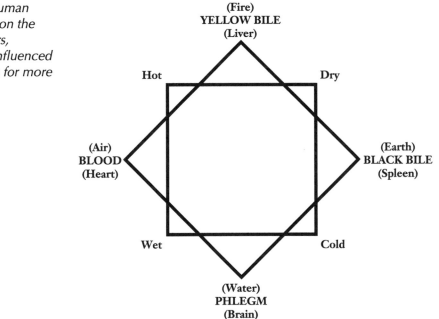

of balance, a person would become ill. Therefore, the goal of many seventeenth-century healers was to keep those humors in balance. Heat, for example, would counterbalance cold; or moisture, dryness. This theory provided the rationale for such standard medical procedures as cutting a person and allowing him or her to bleed for a time or forcing a patient to vomit or sweat heavily.

In the twentieth century, people who are ill expect doctors to make them feel better as soon as possible. In the 1600s, patients expected medicines and treatments to make them feel worse before they were better. If a drug tasted bad or caused unpleasant side effects, then it had to be potent!

During this time, most people still relied on the care and advice of relatives and neighbors in times of illness. A seventeenth-century patient who did consult a doctor would see one of four types of healers: physicians, apothecaries, surgeons, or midwives. Among these four practitioners, physicians were the most respected and usually had the most education. They specialized in treating ailments inside the body, such as fevers or kidney disease, and often prescribed drugs and herbal remedies to their patients.

Apothecaries were the pharmacists of the seventeenth century. But unlike pharmacists today, who are not allowed to prescribe drugs, apothecaries not only prepared drugs and herbal remedies, they also diagnosed patients. People would often ask apothecaries what to take for a certain pain, and they would then be examined and given a recommended drug.

Modern-day artist Robert Thom's rendering of an apothecary at work in his shop in the 1600s

Many physicians did not like apothecaries because the doctors thought that apothecaries did not have adequate training to give medical advice.

Surgeons were the most common healers in the seventeenth century. They performed operations and also treated skin infections and rashes, bled patients, and set broken or fractured bones. Barber-surgeons also cared for patients, although they were often not as well trained as surgeons. In addition, they cut people's hair and pulled their teeth.

Surgeons usually learned their craft by being an apprentice, or helper, to an established surgeon. The surgeon would teach the apprentice everything he knew about surgery. Since drugs to make surgery painless were not yet available, the best surgeons were those who could perform an operation quickly.

During the 1600s, the lines between science, astrology, and magic were often blurred. Although a well-respected physician had spent many years studying at a university, he still might employ such unscientific practices as, for example, reciting a charm as he administered a medication. Or he might consult the stars to find out the best time for treating a patient. At the same time, a healer who practiced magic might also use some of the same methods as the better-trained physicians.

In Europe at that time, women were not licensed to be physicians, apothecaries, or surgeons, although some practiced medicine unofficially. They could, however, be midwives who assisted other women through labor and childbirth. Women had their babies at home, so a midwife might also help with the household tasks while a new mother recovered. Only if the life of both the mother and the child were in danger did a midwife call for the help of a surgeon. The Church bishops licensed midwives, requiring them to be of good character and to baptize infants who appeared unlikely to live long.

Seventeenth-century healers also had few tools to help them treat their patients. They relied on simple surgical knives, herbal medicines, or their own knowledge and experience. Most of the medical instruments that people take for granted today were either not yet invented or yet in use.

For example, in the early 1600s, Italian physician Santorio Santorio designed the mouth thermometer, a device used for measuring a patient's body temperature. Unfortunately, few physicians made use of this tool until the mid-1800s. Another important invention, the microscope, was also developed in the early 1600s. Antony van Leeuwenhoek refined the instrument and, in 1674, while studying a sample of lake water under his microscope, discovered microorganisms, some of which can cause many different ailments in humans and animals. Again, it would be another two hundred years before

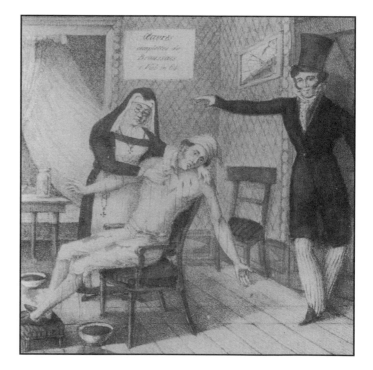

Applying leeches to the skin was a popular blood-letting method used by the ancient Greeks and Romans, as well as Europeans during the Middle Ages. Scientists later discovered that leeches emit a substance in their saliva that prevents blood from clotting in the wound, allowing the blood to flow freely.

the microscope would be used by scientists to find microorganisms responsible for diseases.

This book profiles these innovations and others made during the next 300 years. In 1816, French doctor René Laënnec, too embarrassed to put his ear close to the heart of a woman having chest pains, rolled up a sheaf of papers to form a tube through which he listened to her heart. This simple tool amplified sound so well that he was inspired to make a more complex device from hollowed-out wood. Laënnec called his invention the stethoscope. In 1903, Willem Einthoven invented a machine to measure the electrical impulses, or beats, of the heart, which gave doctors an even more precise way to study and treat this vital organ.

American dentist William T. G. Morton successfully used ether to anesthetize a patient in 1846, making surgery painless. Fifty years later, German physicist Wilhelm Roentgen showed his wife the bones in her hand using a mysterious force he had discovered, which he called the "X" ray. Doctors quickly came to rely on X rays to diagnose patients, and scientists started searching for materials that might emit other powerful rays. Physicist Marie Curie found one—radium—and she and her husband, Pierre, soon discovered that this new element was strong enough to kill living cells, including cancer cells.

These medical innovators of yesterday gave us the life-saving tools—invented the instruments—that patients rely on so heavily today.

CHAPTER ONE

Santorio Santorio and the Thermometer

In the Middle Ages, people understood that a high temperature was a sure sign of illness, and they knew that some fevers were more serious than others. But doctors had difficulty diagnosing fevers because they had no way of measuring the temperature of the body. They could only feel a patient's forehead with their hands to gauge the temperature, a method that was neither accurate nor consistent. One doctor might touch a patient's forehead and say the person had a fever; another might think the patient felt normal. When Santorio Santorio invented the first thermometer in 1612, he gave doctors a much-needed medical tool.

On March 29, 1561, a son, Santorio, was born to Antonio and Elisabetta Santorio. (It was a common practice at the time to give a male child the same first and last name.) The family lived in Capodistria, the capital of Istria, an island in the Adriatic Sea. Santorio had one brother and two

Italian physician Santorio Santorio (1561-1636) devoted his life to accurate scientific measurement and invented many devices to aid his quest for knowledge.

sisters. Antonio was a high official in the republic's military, and Elisabetta came from a family of nobility.

While Santorio was still young, his parents sent him to nearby Venice in Italy to live with the Morosini family. The two families had been friends for many years, and Santorio shared tutors with the Morosini sons. During the time he spent with his foster family, Santorio studied, among other subjects, mathematics, languages, and philosophy. When he turned 14, he entered the University of Padua. A brilliant student, Santorio soon decided on medicine as a career. He spent seven years at the university and began to practice medicine following his graduation in 1582.

Santorio spent the 12 years from 1587 to 1599 somewhere in eastern Europe, although no one knows for certain which country he lived in or why he went there. The University of Padua may have received a letter in 1587 from Count Zrinski in Croatia, inquiring if there was a doctor available to care for him. Other reports say the letter was from Maximillian, the king of Poland. While in eastern Europe, Santorio became known both as an excellent doctor and an inventor. He made devices to measure the speed of wind and the force of currents flowing through water.

Santorio returned to Italy in 1599 because he wanted to be a part of the scientific renaissance that was flourishing there. Scientists from all over the world were gathering to discuss exciting new discoveries. One of the meeting places was the home of his old friends in Venice, the Morosinis.

One of the greatest scientists in Italy at the time was Galileo Galilei, who was a physicist, mathematician, and astronomer. Galileo discovered the moons around the planet Jupiter with a telescope that he had built. He also invented the thermoscope, which measured changes in air temperature. These two pioneers probably met after Santorio had returned to Italy. Although some correspondence from Santorio to Galileo exists, scholars question whether they became friends and shared scientific ideas.

In 1602, Santorio published his first book, *Methodus vitandorum errorum omnium qui in arte medica contigunt* (*Method of Combating All the Errors Which Occur in the Art of Medicine*). The subject of the book was how to avoid making mistakes while practicing medicine. In his book, Santorio quoted at length the Greek physicians Hippocrates and Galen. Sometimes he agreed and sometimes he disagreed with their views.

Santorio's popular book helped him gain a position as a professor of medicine at the University of Padua in 1611. His main duty there was to interpret the teachings of ancient doctors such as Hippocrates. Early in his career, Santorio made known his personal philosophy of medicine:

> One must believe first in one's own senses and in experience, then in reasoning, and only in the third place in the authority of Hippocrates, of Galen, of Aristotle, and of other excellent philosophers.

Hippocrates (460-370 B.C.), considered to be the father of modern medicine, was a Greek physician and teacher.

The medical writings of Greek physician Galen (standing), who lived during the second century, were the ultimate authority for Europeans until the 1600s.

At that time, this philosophy was unusual because most doctors did not dare question the teachings of the ancient physicians.

In 1614, Santorio's most famous book, *Ars de statica medicina (The Art of Static Medicine)*, was published. "Static medicine" was the study of the very old concept of insensible perspiration. The ancient Greeks had noticed that people eat more food than the body gives off as waste. For example, a person might eat three pounds of food and then later excrete a pound of waste. No one could explain what happened to the extra two pounds because people tended to stay at about the same weight.

The Greeks decided that the remaining weight of the consumed food must be lost as invisible sweat through pores in the skin, which they called "insensible perspiration." Santorio wanted to find out how much insensible perspiration a body gave off every day. For several years, he weighed himself carefully before and after every meal by sitting on a large scale. He also weighed his food and compared the amount to the weight of his body waste.

Later, scientists learned that the body simply turns food into energy and burns it off. Santorio's study was important, however, because he was one of the first people to begin using exact measurements in medical experiments. This belief in the value of measurement led him to invent the thermometer.

Santorio Santorio, however, was not the first person to be interested in the measurement of temperature. Although no one knew how to measure a person's body temperature, for many years scientists tried to make devices that would measure the temperature of air or water. Around 100 B.C., Hero of Alexandria's experiments showed that air expands as it heats. Therefore, the same amount, or volume, of warm air takes up more space than air that is cold. For example, a balloon filled with warm air is larger than a balloon filled with the same amount of cold air. Hero's discovery set the stage for the invention of the thermoscope more than 1,700 years later.

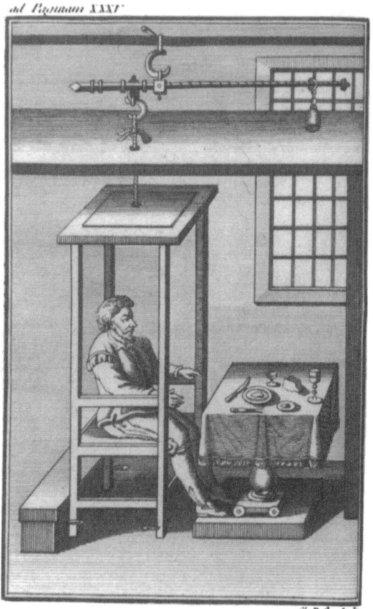

For years, Santorio used this delicate machine called a steelyard to weigh himself before and after meals.

THE BREAKTHROUGH

In the late 1500s, Galileo read about Hero's experiments. He realized that if air volume, the amount of air in some kind of a container, could be measured, then so could air temperature. Galileo built the first working thermoscope. He took a small glass tube filled with air and rubbed it in his hands to warm it up. Then he turned the tube over and put the open end in a small bowl of water. As the air in the tube cooled, water rose into the tube.

Since cooler air takes up less space than warm air, there would be more space for the water as the air in the tube cooled. The water rising slowly in the tube showed that the air was cooling. When Galileo rubbed the glass tube again, the air inside would heat up, and the water level in the tube would slowly drop because the warmer air took up more space than the colder air. Although the increase and decrease could be seen, the thermoscope could not measure the degree of change in a mathematical way.

Despite this lack of precision, Galileo had constructed a wonderful invention. Yet, he considered it to be a useless toy and even called it a "little joke." As far as anyone knows, the famous physicist, mathematician, and astronomer never tried to adapt the thermoscope into a device to measure the temperature of the human body.

It was Santorio Santorio, the physician who had devoted his life to measurements, who realized that he could use the thermoscope to measure body temperature. He made two important changes that

Galileo Galilei (1564-1642), who revealed to the world some startling discoveries in physics and astronomy, lost his own eyesight from many hours of studying sun spots through his telescopes.

transformed Galileo's thermoscope into the thermometer.

Santorio's first innovation was making a glass tube into which a patient could breathe. The person's breath would heat up the air, which would push the water level down inside the tube. (See diagram below.) If the person had a fever, the water level in the tube would be pushed down farther because the patient's breath would be hotter. Santorio colored the water in the tube green so doctors could see it more easily.

Secondly, Santorio added regularly spaced marks, or tick marks, to his device. This may appear to be a very minor addition to Galileo's thermoscope, but it was actually a very important one. With the tick marks, Santorio could get a reading of a patient's temperature and compare this reading to the temperatures of other patients. Or, he could

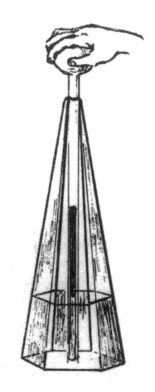

Three types of Santorio thermometers. The device above was grasped by the hand. Also pictured is a thermometer into which the patient breathes and (far right) another that is placed in the mouth.

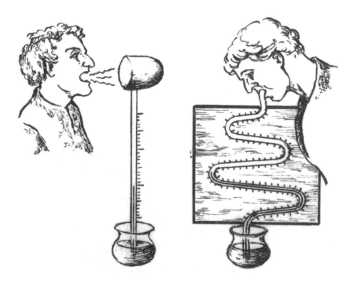

compare the reading to earlier readings taken on the same patient. Santorio knew the thermometer would enable doctors to determine a person's temperature exactly, making both diagnosis and treatment more precise.

After inventing the thermometer, Santorio built a device to measure a person's pulse rate. Today, people can find their pulse rates without special instruments: they only have to count how many times their pulse beats within a certain period of time. Since the clocks of Santorio's day had no second hand, measuring time exactly was difficult.

To solve this problem, Santorio built a pendulum—a weight hanging on the end of a piece of string. Then he matched the swing of the pendulum to a person's pulse rate by changing the length of the cord on which the weight was hanging. He improved this device by tying a knot in the cord and measuring the position of the knot on a horizontal scale. Santorio called this device the pulsilogium.

Among the many other devices Santorio built was a hydroscope, which measured the amount of water in air. To help patients who were paralyzed or had to remain immobile while healing, he invented a bag filled with water in which they could lie and bathe without moving from their bed. He also invented an instrument for removing bladder stones.

Santorio spent so much time treating patients and inventing that his students at the university accused him of not devoting enough time to his teaching. Although these charges were dismissed, Santorio was bitter over the criticism and retired

pendulum: an object suspended from a fixed support that, influenced by gravity, swings freely back and forth; used to regulate devices such as clocks

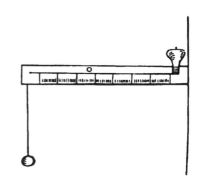

Santorio's sketch of his pulsilogium with a horizontal scale

The word thermometer comes from the Greek words *therme,* meaning heat, and *metron,* meaning a measure.

from the university in 1624. As a reward for his years of outstanding work, however, the Venetian government continued to pay him his university salary for the rest of his life.

In 1630, Venetian officials asked Santorio to organize the efforts of doctors in their city to combat a plague. That same year, Santorio was elected president of the Venetian College of Physicians. On February 22, 1636, Santorio Santorio died from a urinary tract disease and was buried in the Church of the Servi in Venice. When the church was destroyed in 1812 during the Napoleonic Wars, Santorio's skeleton was salvaged, and his skull is now in the museum at the University of Padua.

A wealthy and respected man, Santorio had never married. As he had no family, he willed his money to endow schools and fund other charities and scientific endeavors.

Immediately after his death, Santorio was remembered because of his studies in insensible perspiration, not for inventing the thermometer. When people later understood human metabolism—the process by which the body converts food into energy—they realized that insensible perspiration had been an incorrect theory.

Historian Arturo Castiglioni referred to Santorio as "the first and the most happy innovator" in the field of medicine.

THE RESULT

By the end of the 1600s, the thermometer had become popular, but it was popular as a way to measure air temperature, not as a medical instrument. In the race to build more accurate thermometers, an important discovery was made. People realized that air pressure was always changing, and this rise or fall would affect the accuracy of a thermometer.

In 1641, Ferdinand II, the Grand Duke of Tuscany, solved the problem of changes in air pressure by making a thermometer that was permanently sealed in glass. Thus, air pressure would not affect its accuracy. He also used wine in his thermometer instead of water because wine does not freeze as easily as water. By the end of the century, many thermometer makers were using mercury instead of wine. Mercury, a silvery-colored poisonous element, is the only common metal that is liquid at normal temperatures.

Early in the 1700s, Gabriel Daniel Fahrenheit, a German-Dutch physicist, developed the first standard scale for thermometers. He based his ideas on the work of Danish astronomer Ole Rømer, who was the first person to make a scale based on the freezing and the boiling point of water. On Rømer's scale, water boils at 60° and freezes at 7.5°.

Fahrenheit refined Rømer's scale. On Fahrenheit's scale, water freezes at 32° and boils at 212°, and the average temperature of the human body is 98.6°. In 1742, Anders Celsius, an astronomer from Sweden, developed a scale that was

To devise his temperature scale, Anders Celsius (1701-1744) divided the temperature difference between the boiling and freezing points of water into an even 100 degrees. He initially placed freezing at 100° and boiling at 0°, but he reversed them a year later.

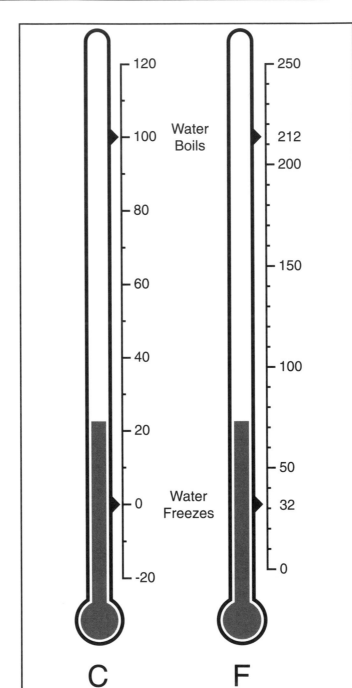

The two most commonly used temperature scales are Celsius (left) and Fahrenheit. As measured on the Celsius scale, water boils at 100° and freezes at 0°. On the Fahrenheit scale, water boils at 212° and freezes at 32°.

easier to use than the Fahrenheit scale. On the Celsius scale, water freezes at 0° and boils at 100°.

The real turning point with regard to the use of thermometers in medicine came in 1868, when a book entitled *The Temperature in Diseases* was published. The author, Carl Wunderlich, a professor of medicine at the University of Leipzig in Germany, recognized that fever was not a disease itself, but a symptom. He collected temperature data from almost 25,000 patients. With his data, he showed how a doctor could use body temperature to diagnose 32 different diseases, including typhus, measles, and pneumonia. Wunderlich's book soon became a guide for doctors in the Western world. Since then, taking a person's temperature has been one of the quickest and easiest ways to determine illness.

In medicine, the enclosed glass thermometer has been largely replaced by the electronic thermometer. Powered by a tiny battery, a heat sensitive device in the tip of the electronic thermometer registers body heat as electrical fluctuations. These fluxes are sent to a computerized sensor, which converts them into temperature readings.

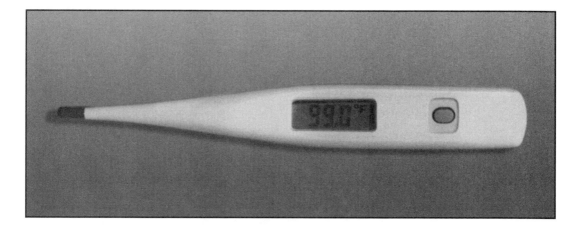

CHAPTER TWO

Antony van Leeuwenhoek and the Microscope

Before scientists had microscopes, no one could actually see the tiny living creatures that exist all around us. These tiny creatures, called microorganisms, are too small to be seen with the human eye. Yet without these creatures, no life would exist on Earth. Microorganisms help dead plants and animals to decay in the soil, making nutrients for new plants to grow. Microorganisms can also make people ill. Bacteria and viruses are types of microorganisms that cause many diseases.

People did not know what caused them to get sick before microorganisms were discovered. Some thought that illness was a punishment from the gods. Others believed that an imbalance of the body's four humors—blood, yellow bile, black bile, and phlegm—caused sickness. After the invention of the microscope, scientists could study microorganisms, including those responsible for diseases. Discovering the cause of a disease is often the first step in finding

Antony van Leeuwenhoek (1632-1723) discovered a previously invisible world when he looked through his microscopes.

a cure. Although Antony van Leeuwenhoek (LAY-ven-hook) did not invent the microscope, he demonstrated to the world what a powerful invention it was.

Antony van Leeuwenhoek was born on October 24, 1632, in Delft, Holland, one of seven children. His father, Philips, was a basket maker. Philips died in 1638 when Antony was only five years old. Two years later, Antony's mother, Margaretha, married a painter named Jacob Molijn. The couple sent Antony, then about seven years old, away to school in the nearby town of Benthuizen, where he lived with an uncle.

After graduating at 16, Antony went to Amsterdam to work as a bookkeeper for a draper (someone who made and sold cloth). He hoped to learn enough about the draper business to pass the standard test that would prove he had mastered the trade. People usually had to study and work for several years to learn enough about business and textiles to pass this test. Leeuwenhoek, however, passed it after working only six weeks at the shop.

In 1654, Leeuwenhoek returned to Delft and opened his own draper shop. That same year, he married Barbara de Mey. Together, Antony and Barbara had five children. Sadly, only one of them, a daughter named Maria, survived to adulthood. Barbara herself died in 1666. In 1671, Leeuwenhoek remarried. He and his second wife, Cornelia Swalmius, had one child, a son, who died in infancy. The death of so many of Leeuwenhoek's children was not unusual during a time when so many diseases that are curable or preventable today were often fatal.

During his first few years back in Delft, Leeuwenhoek became a well-respected businessman. At the age of 27, city officials appointed him to the post of chamberlain to the sheriffs of Delft. In this position, he was responsible for the security and upkeep of the city court and law offices. He hired people to clean and keep the fires lit in the rooms

The great Dutch painter Jan Vermeer, who painted this self-portrait, An Artist in His Studio, *was born in Delft in the same year as Leeuwenhoek. In fact, their births are recorded on the same page of the town's baptismal register. When Vermeer died, leaving little for his family, Leeuwenhoek was appointed executor of the estate and settled Vermeer's financial affairs.*

and to guard the building. He could hold this position while still running his draper business because the job took little time. It was honorable work, however, and it paid well. Leeuwenhoek also spent some time as a surveyor (a person who measures distances and areas, such as parcels of land).

One tool that Leeuwenhoek used often in his fabric business was a magnifying glass. With it, he could check the quality of a piece of fabric. Looking through magnifying glasses fascinated Leeuwenhoek, and this interest later led him to experiment with the more powerful microscope.

Magnifying glasses, microscopes, telescopes, and eyeglasses produce images with lenses. Lenses work by refraction, which is the bending of light rays. This bending happens when the light rays leave one transparent material—glass—and enter another—air. Magnifying glasses, microscopes, and telescopes all use a convex lens, which is a round

A magnifying glass is a large convex lens. When held near a small object, a larger image can be seen in the lens because the lens causes the light rays from the object to converge, or come together, as they enter the eye. The section of the brain that processes vision always assumes that light rays arrive at the eye in straight lines. Therefore, the object is perceived as larger.

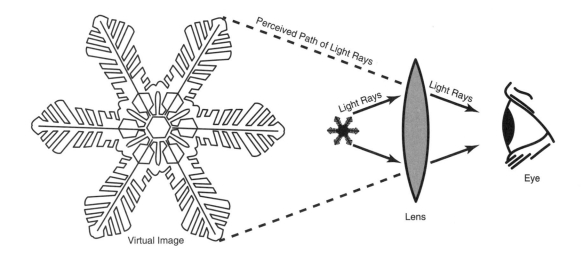

piece of glass that is thicker at the center than at the edges. Light rays from an object pass through the lens and come together on the other side. The object appears larger because the rays enter the eye in a wider angle than they would without the lens.

For thousands of years, people had observed the phenomenon of refraction. Around 150 B.C., the Greek scientist Claudius Ptolemy experimented with a brass rod in a pool of water. The part of the rod that was underwater looked curved, allowing Ptolemy to measure accurately how much the light was bent. Over the next several hundred years, other scientists suggested that it might be possible to use glass to bend light.

Although no one knows who made the first pair of eyeglasses, early records indicate that people were wearing glasses around 1280 in Italy. At first, many people feared glasses because they thought that they were not seeing real things when they looked through lenses. It wasn't long, however, before people realized how useful glasses could be.

concave lens: a round piece of glass that is thicker at the edges than at the center, making light rays diverge, or deflect, in different directions. Objects that these light rays bounce off of appear smaller.

convex lens: a round piece of glass that is thicker at the center than the edges, making light rays converge, or come together, from different directions. Objects that these light rays bounce off of appear larger.

An early advertisement for eyeglasses

An Italian compound microscope used during the 1600s. The eye lens is held inside the draw-tube, which slides over the barrel. The barrel holds a second lens, called the field lens.

The next breakthrough in the use of lenses occurred when Hans Lippershey, a Dutch lens-grinder, held two lenses up to the sky. When he saw the large image they made, he was inspired to put the two lenses together in a tube. He took out a patent for the telescope in 1608. Lippershey, who died about 1619, may also have worked on the compound microscope, which contains two lenses.

Dutchman Zacharias Janssen (1580-1648) was a spectacles maker who is usually credited with developing the compound microscope. Galileo Galilei wrote about Janssen's invention in 1609. The simple, or single-lens, microscope was already in use, although it was not much more powerful than magnifying glasses. Janssen's microscope magnified objects up to nine times as large as they really were because of the two lenses.

In 1625, Francesco Stelluti published *Description of a Bee*, the first scientific study based on the use of a microscope. This book included detailed drawings of a bee's antennae and limbs. While the pictures were interesting, they were not very informative because they did not reveal any more details than people could see by holding up a bee to their eye and squinting. As microscopes improved, scientists began to perform more detailed studies.

THE BREAKTHROUGH

In 1665, British scientist Robert Hooke wrote *Micrographia*, one of the most famous scientific books in history. The Royal Society in England had paid Hooke to examine nature through his microscope and then describe his findings. With his compound microscope that magnified more than 40 times, Hooke could see ordinary objects in great detail. Thus, he was able to make detailed drawings of such varied subjects as moss, fleas, and wine corks. His book caught the imagination of the public because people were fascinated by the incredible detail of his drawings.

A section of *Micrographia* described other microscopes that had not worked very well. One of them was constructed from a piece of broken glass that had been melted into a glass bead. Then wax was used to mount the bead into a small hole in a flat piece of metal. Although this was only a simple microscope, it gave a very clear image. Hooke, however, did not like these little microscopes because "though these are exceedingly easily made, they are yet troublesome to use."

One person who might have read *Micrographia* was Antony van Leeuwenhoek, who may have visited England shortly after the book was published. He knew only Dutch, but perhaps someone translated the book for him. However he acquired the knowledge, Leeuwenhoek built one of Hooke's simple, or single lens, microscopes. Over the course of his lifetime, he would build many more, perhaps 500. He

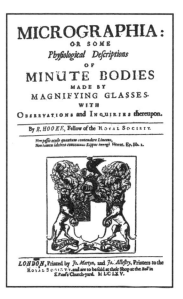

The title page from Robert Hooke's famous book Micrographia, *published in London in 1665*

Antony van Leeuwenhoek examined everything around him, even his own vomit, as he described here: "Soon after I was sick again with great violence, so that the food I brought up (as they told me) came out of my mouth and nose: but I knew not what I was doing. When I came to myself, I examined the stuff I had cast up: and I found it was not only the food I'd taken the evening before, but even what I'd had the previous mid-day."

had a habit of leaving a specimen he liked on the instrument and then making a new one. Obsessive about the quality of his microscopes, Leeuwenhoek took great care in building each one. His instruments were far superior to any others that had been built up to that time. While Hooke's compound microscopes could magnify objects about 40 times, Leeuwenhoek's simple microscopes could magnify up to 500 times!

Leeuwenhoek's simple microscope was superior to Hooke's compound microscope because his lenses were much better. The second lens in the compound microscope not only magnified an image, it also magnified any imperfections of the first lens. Although compound microscopes would eventually be more powerful than simple microscopes, the lenses of the 1600s couldn't provide clear images at that level of magnification.

Leeuwenhoek would spend 10 years learning to craft lenses with few imperfections. He sold his fabric shop and devoted the last 50 years of his life to magnifying everything around him. He examined rain water, animal and human tissues, human sperm and blood, bits of trees and plants, minerals and rocks.

The biggest discovery made by Leeuwenhoek came in August 1674 when he was in a boat on a small lake called Berkelse Mere near his home. The Dutch draper and surveyor knew that the lake water became very cloudy every year in the late summer. No one knew what caused this cloudiness, and Leeuwenhoek wanted to find out. Scooping some lake water into a bottle, he took it home with him. When he looked at the water under one of his microscopes, he was amazed to see tiny creatures swimming around in the water—creatures that were thousands of times smaller than any he had ever seen before! Leeuwenhoek named these miniature creatures "animalcules." Scientists would later refer to them as microorganisms.

Leeuwenhoek became well known for his discoveries and was visited by many famous people of

These animalcules had different colors, some being whitish and transparent, others with green and very glittering little scales; yet others were green in the middle and white at both ends, and some were grey, like ash. And the motion of most of these tiny creatures in the water was so fast, and so random, upwards, downwards and round in all directions, that it was truly wonderful to see.
—Antony van Leeuwenhoek

the day, including kings and queens and Tsar Peter the Great of Russia. Hating to be interrupted in his work, he would sometimes not even greet a visitor. He once wrote, "But if I should receive everyone who comes to my house, or tries to come, I should have no freedom at all, but be quite a slave."

When Leeuwenhoek did let people see his collection, he would only show them certain microscopes. He refused to sell any of his instruments, and he never wrote down his method or trained anyone to make lenses as precisely as he did.

There are, however, detailed records of his work. Elected a fellow of the Royal Society in England in 1680, Leeuwenhoek wrote hundreds of letters to the Society, translated from Dutch to English by friends. Upon his election, the Society presented him with a medal inscribed in Latin, *"In tenui labor, at tennuis non gloria."* This translates, "His work was in little things, but not little in glory." He also willed a case of his microscopes, with specimens attached, to the Royal Society.

Leeuwenhoek lived to be more than 90 years old and experimented on microscopes to the end of his life. During his last days, he was examining some sand that the East India Company had sent him, wanting to know if he could find gold in the sand with a microscope. Before he could finish this task, Antony van Leeuwenhoek died on August 26, 1723.

Antony van Leeuwenhoek allows a visitor to peer through some of his microscopes (left). Although he made hundreds of them, only nine original microscopes are known to exist, including the one pictured below.

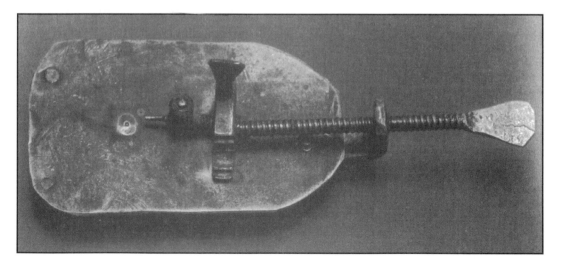

Louis Pasteur (1822-1895) advised scientists and doctors to "find the germ. Then turn it into a vaccine for the patient." The microscope was one of the most important tools that scientists used for discovering germs.

THE RESULT

The next big innovation in microscopes did not happen for more than 100 years. In 1830, J. J. Lister developed an achromatic lens, a combination of lenses made of different kinds of glass. These lenses improved the images seen with earlier compound microscopes and made the microscopes easier to manufacture.

Throughout the 1800s, microscope technology advanced rapidly. As people became better at grinding lenses, microscopes became increasingly powerful. Late in the nineteenth century, the French scientist Louis Pasteur stunned the world when, with the help of his microscope, he proved that tiny microorganisms cause many diseases. (Two centuries before, Leeuwenhoek had observed some of the same tiny organisms swimming in water.) Understanding the cause of a disease enabled Pasteur and others to find new cures for them.

By the end of the nineteenth century, scientists knew that simple and compound microscopes were capable of only limited magnification. No matter how good their lenses, traditional microscopes could magnify an object only a certain number of times. In order to see even more detail, twentieth-century inventors had to devise a new kind of microscope—the electron microscope.

Ernst Ruska and Max Knoll built the first electron microscope in 1932. Traditional microscopes can magnify objects up to approximately 2,000 times. An electron microscope, however, can magnify an object up to 1 million times. Electron microscopes use a beam of moving electrons instead of light. This beam strikes a specimen, which deflects the electrons and, with the aid of a magnetic projector in the microscope, forms an electron image on a fluorescent screen.

Scientists continue to invent new kinds of microscopes that have the potential to magnify objects more easily and cheaply than electron microscopes. Some of these new microscopes use X rays, and others use sound waves. Whatever its form, the microscope continues to be a valuable instrument for both doctors and scientists.

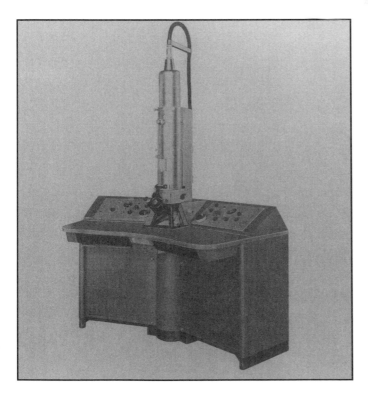

The electron microscope produces an image with a beam of electrons.

CHAPTER THREE

René T. H. Laënnec and the Stethoscope

Two thousand years ago, Hippocrates (or perhaps one of his students) wrote that a person listening to someone else's chest could hear distinct sounds. For instance, if the lungs were filled with fluid, a person would hear a noise that "bubbles like boiling vinegar." An injured lung might "creak like new leather."

It was difficult to hear those sounds in a patient's chest, however, until the stethoscope was invented some 200 years ago by René Laënnec (Re-NAY Lah-en-NEK). This wonderful device allows modern-day doctors to hear a heart beat and the lungs breathe. Today, patients can hardly imagine a doctor without a stethoscope hanging around his or her neck.

René Théophile Hyacinthe Laënnec, the oldest of three children, was born on February 17, 1781, in the small town of Quimper, France. His mother, Michelle, died when he was only six years old. His

"Health, a treasure appreciated only after it has left us," wrote French physician René Théophile Hyacinthe Laënnec (1781-1826), who was often ill and died at the age of 45.

father, Théophile, was a lawyer who wanted to be a poet. Théophile had little interest in caring for his three children after his wife's death. He sent René and his younger brother, Michaud, to live with their uncle, Guillaume Laënnec, in Nantes, France, and René's sister, Marie Ann, went to stay with her great aunt, Madame de la Potterie. Guillaume Laënnec, a very intelligent and hardworking doctor, influenced his nephews greatly. Without his uncle's guidance, René might never have become a doctor.

Life was hard in France at the end of the 1700s. A bloody revolution disrupted the country as people rebelled against their king, Louis XVI. Angered by years of poverty and political repression, French rebels executed many aristocrats and their suspected sympathizers. Despite the political turmoil, René continued with his schooling. He was an excellent student and looked ahead to the day when he would be a doctor like his uncle.

Laënnec was often ill and for most of his life fought against tuberculosis. Tuberculosis, or TB, is a highly contagious disease that damages the lungs. A person with TB tires easily, runs a fever, coughs up mucus, and can be ill for many years before dying.

Still, in April 1801, Laënnec was able to set out for Paris to study medicine. Because the capital of France was one of the best cities in which to study medicine, this adventure would be his big chance to achieve his dream. The French Revolution had finally ended, and people were moving to Paris to find jobs and make new lives for themselves. As the city grew, there was a great need for more doctors.

Although Paris was 200 miles away from Nantes, Laënnec walked most of the way.

Laënnec began his studies at a hospital named the Charité. Laënnec could not have picked a better place to study. Most European hospitals of the period were unhealthy places that packed five or six ill people together in one bed. The Charité, however, was an advanced hospital, with one patient to a bed, and the caretakers kept the facility clean and bright.

Medical students at this time read very little. Instead, they learned by watching and listening while working in the hospital. Laënnec and the other students would follow a professor around the Charité to see the patients. Each day, the professor would examine the patients and tell the students about different ways of treating the varied symptoms they observed. Then Laënnec and the other students

Most hospitals in Laënnec's time were dark, old, and dirty. Often sick people would wake up in the morning to find that one or more people who shared the bed with them had died during the night.

Considered the founder of pathology, Giovanni Battista Morgagni (Mawr-GAH-nyee) (1682-1771) performed 640 autopsies during his nearly 60 years as a professor of anatomy at the University of Padua in Italy.

autopsy: an examination of a body after death has occurred to determine the cause of death, or the extent of injuries, or the progress of a disease. Dissection and other methods are used.

would meet in a classroom and talk about the patients they had seen.

Students also learned medicine by watching professors dissect dead bodies. Because he loved research, Laënnec performed hundreds of autopsies, examining how different deadly diseases affected each organ. Until 1761, doctors had thought that diseases always affected the entire body. Then Giovanni Morgagni published his findings about how some diseases affect only certain organs. One disease that Laënnec studied was peritonitis. His discovery that peritonitis destroys the linings of organs in the body added more evidence to support Morgagni's theory.

While many of these students had classes in only the basic medical subjects, Laënnec wanted to know more. So he studied physics and chemistry and also learned Latin and Greek because one of his goals was to read the writings of Hippocrates in the original Greek. He even took art and music lessons and learned to play the flute. While he was still a student, Laënnec began to publish scientific papers in medical journals.

After graduating from medical school, Laënnec set up his own private practice. He was well respected as a doctor and had more patients than he could handle. In 1816, Laënnec became physician-in-chief at Hôpital Necker, a small hospital outside of Paris, and it was here that he made his great discovery.

THE BREAKTHROUGH

Laënnec may never have developed the stethoscope without the work of Leopold Auenbrugger, a doctor who was practicing in the 1700s. Born in 1722 in Austria, Auenbrugger was the son of an innkeeper. As a boy, he had worked for his father at the inn. He may have learned to determine how much beer was left in a keg by tapping it and listening to the sound it made. Where filled with beer, the keg sounded flat; where empty, the keg gave a deep hollow sound.

When he became a doctor, Auenbrugger used similar skills to examine a patient's chest. He discovered that by tapping a patient on the chest, he could hear different sounds. For example, some diseases cause the lungs to fill with fluid. Lungs filled with fluid make a different sound from lungs that are clear and healthy. Auenbrugger's practice of tapping the chest and listening to the sounds is called percussion.

Auenbrugger wrote a book about his discovery, but it was ignored until 1808 when a doctor named Jean-Nicolas Corvisart translated it from German to French and popularized the method. Corvisart, one of Laënnec's teachers, taught the young doctor about percussion. So by the time Laënnec officially began his work at Necker on September 4, 1816, he knew about Auenbrugger's work.

On September 13, Laënnec examined a patient who was having chest pains. Laënnec feared that something was wrong with the woman's heart. Unfortunately, this woman was quite overweight, so

percussion: a method of medical diagnosis in which the examiner taps a person's chest, back, or abdomen to determine the condition of the body organs in the area, such as the lungs

Jean-Nicolas Corvisart could easily have claimed Leopold Auenbrugger's lost art of percussion to be his own invention when he translated the work, but he said of the Austrian doctor: "It is he and the beautiful invention which rightly belongs to him that I wish to recall to life."

Leopold Auenbrugger (1722-1809) was physician-in-chief at the Hospital of the Holy Trinity in Vienna, Austria. He used his percussion methods to diagnose his patients and confirmed his results by performing autopsies on those who had died.

percussion did not work because fat deadened the sound. In such cases, doctors would often put their ears to a patient's chest and listen, but Laënnec was too embarrassed to put his ear on the woman's chest. He had to find another way to listen to her heart.

According to a story about Laënnec's discovery, an idea came to him shortly after seeing this patient. While he was walking through a garden thinking about her, he saw two boys playing a game that he had played as a child. Each boy stood at one end of a long piece of wood and held it up to his ear. Using a pin, one boy scratched the wood. The other boy listened through the wood and heard the scratching loud and clear. As Laënnec watched the boys, he suddenly realized that if the scratching sound traveled clearly through wood, then sounds from the human chest might also travel through wood. He rushed back to the hospital to try out his theory on the young woman.

Whether or not this story is true, Laënnec suddenly realized that if he listened through an object, the sounds in the chest would be amplified, or made louder, making them easier to hear. He rolled up a sheaf of papers and placed one end of the paper tube on the chest of his patient. When he listened to the other end, the thumping sounds of her heart came through loud and clear. This rolled-up stack of papers was the world's first stethoscope.

I took some sheets of paper and, rolling them very tightly, I applied one end to the precordial regions and placing my ear at the other end, I was as surprised as I was gratified to hear the beating of the heart much more clearly and distinctly than if I had applied my ear directly to the chest. It occurred to me that this means could become a useful method.

—René Laënnec

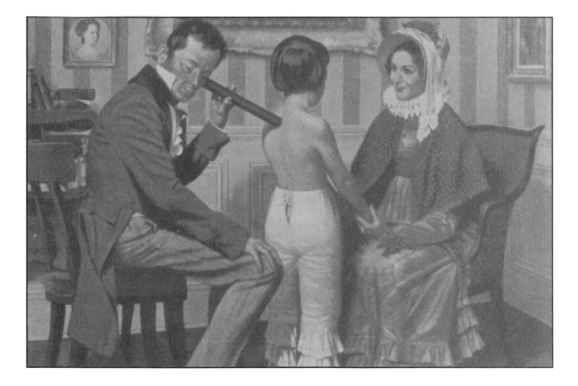

THE RESULT

Laënnec knew right away that his discovery was important. Doctors could use the stethoscope not only to listen to the heart but also to the lungs to hear abnormal sounds or to determine why a patient was having trouble breathing. With practice, Laënnec himself could diagnose various diseases simply by listening through his stethoscope.

At first, Laënnec's stethoscope consisted of paper tied up with pieces of string. He soon tired of tying up stacks of paper, so he tried to make a stethoscope out of wood. Using a lathe, he made cylinders from wood and quickly discovered that he obtained the best sound from a human body when the stethoscope had a hollow channel running through the center.

Through repeated experimentation, Laënnec determined that stethoscopes made from light woods, especially beech, worked better than those formed from ebony, metal, or glass. Soon he was making two-piece stethoscopes that doctors could take apart and put back together for easy carrying.

Laënnec decided to call his invention the stethoscope. This name comes from the Greek words *stethos*, which means "chest," and *skopein*, which means "to examine." Other people called the stethoscope a pectoriloquy, a baton, a solometer, or a medical trumpet. Laënnec sometimes simply called it "the cylinder." He named the process of using a stethoscope "ausculation," a word derived from Latin and meaning "to listen carefully."

ausculation: the act of listening for sounds made by internal organs during an examination

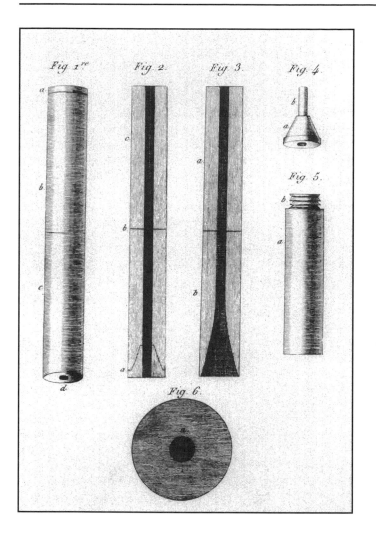

Laënnec's wooden stethoscope is shown fully assembled (Figure 1) and dismantled (Figures 2-5). Part (a) was placed on the patient's chest, and the opposite end (c) was put against the physician's ear. Figure 6 shows a cross-section of the cylinder and its hollow center.

By August 1819, Laënnec had written a two-volume book entitled *On Mediate Ausculation, or a Treatise on the Diagnosis of Diseases of the Lungs and Heart Based Principally on the New Method of Investigation.* Between treating his patients, doing research, teaching students, and writing his book, Laënnec was exhausted. He had never enjoyed good

Laënnec also became famous for identifying tuberculosis. Doctors knew tubercles—small, round knots of tissue caused by bacteria—occurred on many different body organs. Laënnec theorized that a lung disease known as phthisis, or consumption, was actually caused by tubercles on the lungs. This disease has been called pulmonary tuberculosis since a lecture he gave in 1804. He may have contracted tuberculosis from one of the many autopsies he performed.

health, and now he was on the verge of collapse. After finishing his book, he decided to retire to the country to regain his strength. Two years passed before he was healthy enough to return to his work in Paris.

Laënnec arrived in Paris late in 1821 and accepted a position as a professor at the Collège de France. There, he spent most of his time working at the Charité, where he had earlier been a medical student. Many honors were offered to him, and he was elected to the Academy of Medicine in 1823. A year later, he was made a Knight of the French Legion of Honor.

René Laënnec married Jacqueline Argou in December 1824. His wife became pregnant the following spring, and Laënnec, who was now in his forties, was ecstatic about finally becoming a father. Sadly, Jacqueline miscarried a few months later, which was a devastating loss for them. Shortly after, the hard-working doctor suffered a recurrence of tuberculosis. Laënnec soon resigned his position at the university and headed back to the country to regain his strength. But he was there for only a few months before he died on August 13, 1826.

After Laënnec's death, new stethoscopes were developed. Doctors in England found the short wooden tube to be awkward, so they came up with a longer, more flexible version. Many other European countries began to use the British version of the stethoscope instead of Laënnec's original design.

An American doctor in New York, George Philip Camman, made the first modern binaural stethoscope in 1855. (Binaural means that someone can listen with both ears.) This innovation made hearing the sounds inside the chest much easier. Camman's stethoscope was the model for those used by doctors everywhere today.

The stethoscope is still the most widely used bedside instrument. Doctors know that before they can cure patients, they must find out what is wrong with them. Stethoscopes are one of the most important tools they use in their diagnosis.

A twentieth-century doctor using a modern stethoscope

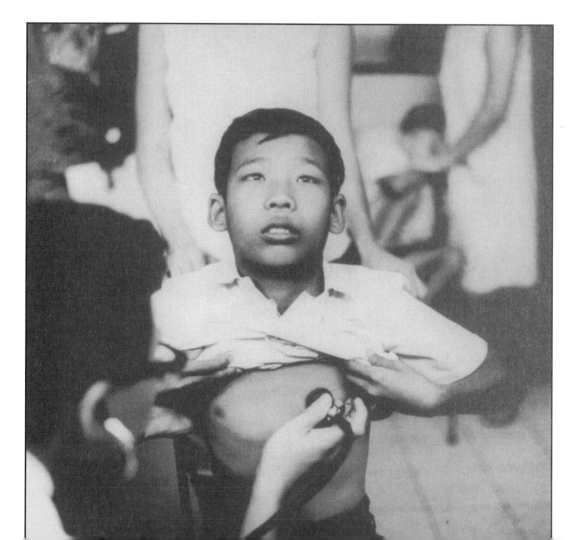

CHAPTER FOUR

William T. G. Morton and Anesthetics

In 1845, a student at Harvard Medical School named William T. G. Morton watched as a doctor demonstrated modern surgery to the class. The patient, a 50-year-old man, had an infected leg that had to be amputated to keep the infection from spreading to the rest of his body. Painkillers, also called anesthetics, were not yet in use, so the doctor had strapped the patient down to a table, hoping for the best.

The patient's breathing grew louder as he watched the doctor lower the knife. He screamed in agony as the doctor cut skillfully into his leg. The patient's face turned purple, and tears and sweat ran down his cheeks. Finally, the patient fainted with pain, and the doctor finished the operation.

Less than two years following that operation, Morton revealed to the world a procedure that would spare patients the terrible pain of surgery. He discovered how to administer anesthetics.

The use of ether by American dentist William Thomas Green Morton (1819-1868) ushered in a new age in surgery.

William Thomas Green Morton was born in Charlton, Massachusetts, in 1819. William's great-great-great-grandfather, Robert Morton, had come to America from Scotland in 1700 and acquired thousands of acres of land in New Jersey. By 1819, when William was born, the state government no longer recognized the Morton claim to this land, so he grew up on a farm in a poor family.

In 1840, at the age of 21, Morton attended the Baltimore College of Dental Surgery in Maryland. The school had opened that same year, and it was the first dental college in the world. At the time, many people did not think highly of dentists. Most dentists were not well educated, and few were skilled.

In 1843, Morton became partners with Horace Wells, a dentist practicing in Hartford, Connecticut, who had written a textbook on dentistry when he was 23. The two men established an office in Boston. Although they advertised their services in the newspaper, business was slow for Wells and Morton. A patient who came to their office because his false teeth were painful gave Morton an idea for saving their practice.

Morton was sure that better false teeth existed than those in the mouth of his patient. Boston dentists made false teeth from hippopotamus teeth (which are actually ivory tusks that grow throughout the animal's life) and glued them to the roots of the patient's real teeth. Springs held the false teeth in place. Unfortunately, the teeth decayed quickly, and the glue turned black after being in the mouth for only a short time.

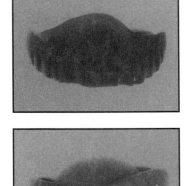

Examples of other types of false teeth, or dentures, in use during the 1850s

Wanting to help his patient, Morton looked in one of his textbooks and found instructions for making teeth out of powdered feldspar, a common white mineral. Following the instructions, Morton and Wells mixed the feldspar with metallic oxides until it resembled a flour paste. Then they pressed the paste into molds. They baked the teeth several times and then enameled them by hand. The key to making a good set of false teeth, the text explained, was pulling out the roots of the decayed teeth instead of attaching the false teeth to the old roots. Then the false teeth were cemented to a gold plate that fitted over the gums.

Morton was excited about the possibilities of this technique. By making the best false teeth available, he thought that he and Wells would become rich men. The young dentist dreamed that one day they would have to build their own denture factory to meet the demand for their false teeth.

It was at this time that Morton and Wells met Charles Jackson, a noted Boston chemist. Jackson agreed to test the solder, or cement, the two dentists used to glue the teeth to the gold plate. Jackson made some suggestions, and together the three men devised a formula strong enough to hold the false teeth in place.

To inform the public about their new denture-making process, Morton advertised that he and Wells would fit a person with a set of false teeth for only the cost of the teeth. If the patient were perfectly satisfied with the dentures after using them for a year, only then would the dentists charge a fee

feldspar: a group of common rock-forming minerals that consists of aluminum with potassium, sodium, and calcium

for their services. At this point, Wells got cold feet and quit the partnership. He called the venture "madness" and returned to Hartford. Morton continued without him.

Within a few weeks, word got around about how good Morton's false teeth were. Every day, well-to-do middle-aged men and women seeking better dentures crowded into his office. By February 1844, only four months after he had set his plan in motion, Morton had hired two assistants and started to build his tooth factory. He had so many patients that he had to turn away some of them.

For more than a year, Morton had been courting a woman named Elisabeth Whitman, who came from a rich family in Connecticut. Her parents did not like Morton because his family was poor, and

Shortly after Horace Wells (1815-1848) dissolved his partnership with William Morton, the denture business they had started became successful.

they thought their daughter could do better than marry a mere dentist. In spite of their disapproval, Morton had visited Whitman whenever he could, and her parents slowly realized that he was honest and respectable. When Morton was finally able to show Whitman's parents that he was succeeding as a dentist, they agreed to let their daughter marry him. The wedding took place on May 29, 1844.

In the beginning, life went smoothly for the young dentist. His denture business continued to prosper, and his marriage was a happy one. The only dark cloud in his sky was the pain that his patients felt when he fitted them for their false teeth. In order for the dentures to fit correctly, Morton had to pull his patients' teeth. Because no painkilling drugs were available, the patients suffered greatly when he wrenched the teeth from their sockets.

The screams of his patients haunted Morton. The only relief he could offer was whiskey, wine, or laudanum, an opium-based drug. If the patients were drunk or drugged, they did not feel the pain quite as much. Still, Morton sought a better way to help his patients. He did not like to think of them experiencing so much pain, and he knew he could not go on listening to their screams for the rest of his working life. Shortly before getting married, Morton decided to attend nearby Harvard Medical School, which was one of the finest medical schools in the world. From the surgeons there who operated on patients on a regular basis, he surely would discover how to keep his patients from feeling such intense pain.

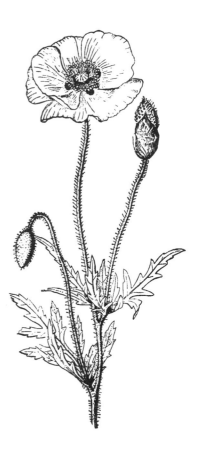

Opium, the sticky extract of the poppy plant (shown above), had been used in Asia where poppies are native. Laudanum was a mixture of opium and alcohol commonly used as a painkiller in the United States during the 1800s.

Charles Thomas Jackson (1805-1880) obtained a medical degree from Harvard, but he practiced for only five years. His family had come to the United States on the Mayflower, *and the philosopher and writer Ralph Waldo Emerson was his brother-in-law.*

THE BREAKTHROUGH

To prepare for classes in the autumn, Morton went back to Dr. Charles Jackson, the chemist who had helped him and Wells some months earlier. Morton felt fortunate that Jackson agreed to tutor him in chemistry. Jackson was an experienced teacher and also a high-ranking member of scientific societies around the world. Years later, however, Morton would regret ever having met Jackson.

Morton soon learned that the chemist was a difficult man who was infamous for taking credit for research done by his students and even by other scientists. Students told Morton how Jackson had unfairly tried to take credit for the telegraph that Samuel Morse had invented. Even though Jackson could be demanding and dishonest, he was still a fine teacher and taught Morton a great deal.

One day while the two men were discussing the distillation of ether, a liquid mixture of ethyl alcohol and sulfuric acid, Jackson mentioned that some students at Harvard had parties and sniffed ether. If they inhaled too much, the fumes first made them giddy and then unconscious.

Intrigued, Morton began to research ether. The substance had first been synthesized by Valerius Cordus in the 1500s. Although used to reduce pain or fever, no one had recognized its anesthetic property. By the 1800s, many doctors, including Jackson, mistrusted the substance, saying that ether was dangerous because it was flammable, and it could be deadly if a doctor gave a patient too much.

Despite the dangers, Morton tried "toothache drops" of ether on one of his patients who had a tooth so sore and sensitive that she nearly fainted whenever he touched it. Soaking the tooth in ether deadened the pain and allowed him to operate. With other patients, however, the substance had no effect, or it actually caused more pain.

Early in January 1845, Morton received a letter from his former partner, Horace Wells, describing a lecture he had attended in December. At this presentation, a man was demonstrating the effects of breathing nitrous oxide. He inhaled so much of this "laughing gas" that he injured himself by stumbling around and falling off the stage. After recovering, he insisted that he had felt no pain when he hit the floor. The incident aroused Wells's interest.

The day following the lecture, Wells had one of his own teeth pulled while breathing nitrous oxide. Feeling no pain at all, Wells was sure he was on to something. Morton arranged for Wells to demonstrate his discovery in front of the doctors and students in Morton's anatomy class at Harvard. The doctors were skeptical of the procedure, but they politely watched as he prepared a young patient to have a tooth pulled. The boy breathed in the nitrous oxide, but Wells removed the gas bag too soon. When Wells pulled on the tooth, the patient howled with pain. The medical students grumbled and booed at the dentist for wasting their time. He left in disgrace and soon gave up dentistry.

Morton was shaken by what had happened to Wells in front of the doctors at Harvard. Still, he

ether: a liquid mixture of ethyl alcohol and sulfuric acid. It is sweet smelling and highly flammable, and inhaling the fumes can induce unconsciousness.

nitrous oxide: a light anesthetic gas mixture of nitrogen and oxygen (N_2O) used today primarily by dentists

Nitrous oxide was discovered in 1772 by Joseph Priestley (1733-1804), an English scientist and clergyman. Priestley also discovered oxygen. In 1795, Humphry Davy was the first to inhale nitrous oxide. The gas made Davy feel giddy and relaxed his muscles, so he called it "laughing gas."

The pain associated with dentistry had changed little between the time of this illustration (about 1650) and when Morton began his practice almost 200 years later.

was determined to find a way to save people from the intense pain of operations because the screams of his patients echoed in his head. In fact, the need to find a good painkiller for his patients took over his life. His wife, Elisabeth, thought that he was spending far too much time away from her and their young son, Willie.

Now Morton began to experiment on himself. He would pour some ether on a rag and breathe until he felt lightheaded. He also worked with birds, insects, and even goldfish, giving them ether to see how it affected them. But most of his testing was done either on himself or his dog. He found that he could put his spaniel to sleep for several minutes with ether. Soon he was spending so much time experimenting with ether that he asked another dentist, Granville Hayden, to run his dentistry office.

The next step was to try ether on another human being. At first, he asked his assistants, Tom Spear and William Leavitt, to find people on the street and offer them $5 (then a large sum of money) to allow him to put them under with ether. No one would agree to try his experiment. Finally, Spear and Leavitt permitted Morton to experiment on them. Carefully, he had them inhale ether. But instead of becoming calm and sleepy, the assistants became aggressive and angry.

This result alarmed Morton because it was the exact opposite of what he had expected. After further testing, he discovered that the ether he was using was not pure. Before continuing to work with people, he would have to find a source of pure ether.

Hayden, his fellow dentist, suggested that Morton contact Charles Jackson, the chemist who had helped Morton before, about a source for ether. Although Morton remembered that Jackson was known for claiming credit for other people's inventions, he decided to talk to him anyway.

Jackson gave Morton the names of people from whom he could buy pure ether. But the chemist also told Morton that giving ether to patients was foolish. It would never work, he said, and it might even be dangerous. Morton simply thanked Jackson for his advice.

When he arrived back at the office with a new supply of ether, Morton noticed the glass inhaler he had recently hired a local manufacturer to make for

The glass inhaler William Morton designed for administering ether

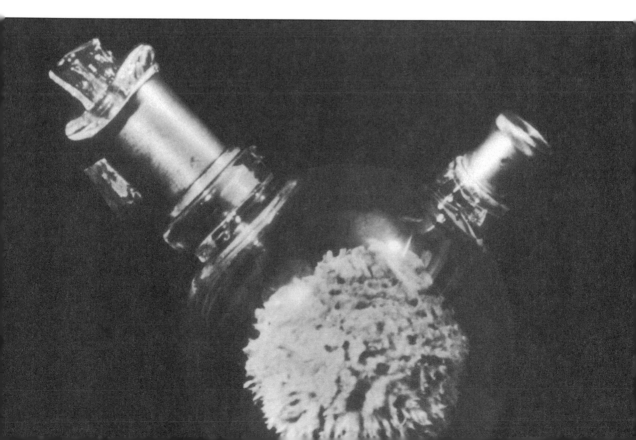

him. Deciding to test the new system on himself, he saturated a sponge with ether, dropped the sponge into the glass globe, and sat down. Glancing at his watch to check the time, he breathed deeply through the tube attached to the glass inhaler. About eight minutes later, he came to. When he first awoke, his legs were numb, but this passed, and he suffered no other ill effects. Confident that with the inhaler and this pure ether he could now treat patients without harming them, Morton decided to find a patient the next day who would agree to try the ether.

Late that night, a man rapped on his door. Eben Frost was suffering from a terrible toothache and in great pain. Morton excitedly explained that he could pull the tooth without pain if Frost would agree to try something new. Frost was grateful for anything that would reduce his pain and willingly agreed. He inhaled ether and was soon oblivious to everything around him. When he came to, his tooth was gone, and he said he had felt no pain. The experiment amazed Frost, who told everyone he knew about this wonderful discovery. Word of Morton's achievement spread quickly.

Morton knew that ether had great potential and that doctors could use it for any kind of operation. Knowing that this would be the true test of ether, he set up a demonstration at Massachusetts General Hospital.

The demonstration took place on October 16, 1846. His 20-year-old patient, Gilbert Abbott, had a three-inch tumor imbedded in his neck. The operation was performed by John Collins Warren,

one of the top surgeons in the United States. Because the patient was breathing ether, he felt nothing as Warren successfully removed the tumor.

When the operation was over, Warren looked at the amazed crowd assembled at the hospital and proclaimed, "Gentlemen, this is no humbug."

This 1893 painting, Ether Day *by Robert Hinckley, depicts the world's first surgery using anesthesia. Surgeon John Collins Warren is directly behind the patient; Morton holds the inhaler. Artist Hinckley spent 10 years researching and painting this work.*

A new era has opened on the operating surgeon. His visitations on the most delicate parts are performed, not only without the agonizing screams he has been accustomed to hear, but sometimes in a state of perfect insensibility, and, occasionally, even with an expression of pleasure on the part of the patient.
—John Collins Warren

THE RESULT

News of the effectiveness of ether spread around the world. Although many doctors still considered the substance to be dangerous, they now began to realize how valuable ether was if used with care.

Morton applied to the U.S. government for a patent on the method of administering ether and for his inhaler. Sulfuric ether was a common substance, but if Morton had a patent on the method, people would have to purchase his inhaler and instructions on how to use ether. Thus, his discovery would not only earn him money but would also ensure that ether was administered safely. (Morton knew that ether could be deadly if it were not used with caution.)

Before the government awarded the patent, Charles Jackson visited Morton to remind him that he had given Morton advice on using ether. The chemist demanded $500 from Morton plus a small percentage of the profits. If Morton met these two conditions, the chemist promised to let Morton make all the decisions about how ether should be used. Remembering that Jackson liked to take credit for the discoveries of others, Morton was relieved this was all that Jackson wanted, and he quickly agreed to his demands. The U.S. government awarded Morton his patent for the use of ether.

Then news came that Charles Jackson had sent a letter to the French Academy of Sciences, claiming credit for the discovery of ether as an anesthetic. Moreover, Jackson was telling all his fellow scientists in the United States that he was the true discoverer. He compared himself to Christopher Columbus and Morton to one of Columbus's sailors.

Even though many scientists in the Boston area, including the famous doctor and poet Oliver Wendell Holmes, supported Morton, many scientists worldwide believed Jackson's claims. After all, Jackson was famous. He was well educated and had published many papers during his lifetime. These scientists had never heard of Morton, who had little formal education and had never been published. As the controversy increased, people stopped coming to Morton's dental office.

Another person also claimed to have discovered inhalation anesthesia. A party amusement of the time was sniffing ether, and Dr. Crawford Long of Jefferson, Georgia, noticed that people injured during these "ether frolics" felt no pain. So, on March 30, 1842, he had used ether in an operation to remove a tumor from a patient's neck, but he had not published his results until 1849. Although urged by his friends to contest Morton's patent, Long never pressed hard for recognition.

Horace Wells, however, felt betrayed by his former partner. During 1847, he published many articles claiming that the use of ether and nitrous oxide had been his idea, and he hired attorneys to help him legally claim priority. Distraught and perhaps drunk or drugged, on January 23, 1848, he threw acid on two women and was arrested. That night, after writing letters to his wife and to the press, he anesthetized himself with the chloroform

In addition to supporting Morton's claim of discovery of ether as a painkiller, Oliver Wendell Holmes named the new procedure. "The state should, I think, be called anesthesia. This signifies insensibility. . . . The adjective will be anesthetic," he wrote to Morton on November 21, 1846.

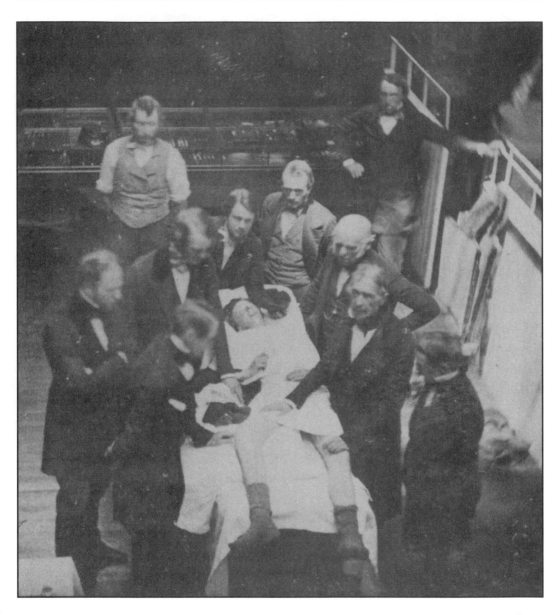

This daguerreotype was made on October 17, 1846, at the second operation performed with the use of ether anesthesia. Unnerved by the sight of blood, photographer Josiah Hawes had failed to take any photographs of the first surgery the previous day. The surgeon, John Collins Warren, stands in the right foreground, his hands on the patient. William Morton, wearing a the checked vest, stands behind the operating table.

with which he had been experimenting, and he fatally cut open a vein in his leg.

About this time, Morton also stopped earning money from his patent. The United States was at war with Mexico. Although Morton had offered his method to the military free of charge and the purchase of his inhalers at cost, both the army and the War Department had refused, saying ether would be too difficult to use in the field hospitals. But army doctors were using ether anyway, and because the army had not obtained permission from Morton, no one else felt they should either. Many doctors who had purchased the rights from Morton now demanded that he return their money.

Morton, who was using all of his time and energy fighting Jackson's claim to ether, could not fight back against the infringement of his patent, and he quickly fell into debt. The people and doctors of Boston collected $1,000 to help and presented him their donation in a silver box that bore the inscription, "He has become poor in a cause which has made the world his debtor."

Despite the help of his Boston friends and the support of his wife's family, Morton sank deeper into debt. He had little recourse but to go to Congress and argue that he should be given money to support himself and his family, especially since the U.S. Army was responsible for the loss of money from his patent. Several times, Morton and his supporters came close to convincing Congress to grant him money, but each time his case became lost in all the other important bills before the assembly at the time,

> Oh! my dear wife and child, whom I leave destitute of the means of support—I would still live and work for you, but I cannot—for if I were to live on, I should become a maniac. I feel that I am one already.
> —Horace Wells's suicide note

The invention of surgical anesthesia was the first major contribution that American medical science made to the world. To this day, it remains our greatest gift to the art of healing. —Sherwin B. Nuland in *Doctors: The Biography of Medicine*

including expansion into the western territories and the problem of slavery.

Soon Morton, like Wells, gave up dentistry. The fight with Jackson had exhausted him and had left him in poor health, even though he was not yet 30 years old. Because he and Elisabeth had three children to care for and little money coming in, Morton took up farming.

Morton's only real later success came during the Civil War (1861-1865) when he worked with army doctors on the battlefields, giving ether to wounded soldiers. Everyone he met showed him respect when they learned that he was the dentist who had discovered how to administer anesthetics.

Following the war, Morton lived simply on his farm. Occasionally, scientists and politicians would convince him to go to Washington, D.C., to fight for the recognition he deserved. In the summer of 1868, he traveled to New York City to speak with an editor of *Atlantic Monthly*, a magazine that had published an article in June supporting Jackson's claims to the ether discovery. While there, he became ill and died on July 15 at the age of 48. His tombstone was inscribed:

> William T. G. Morton, inventor and revealer of Anaesthetic Inhalation. By whom pain in surgery was averted and annulled. Before whom in all time, surgery was agony. Since whom science has control of pain.

Ironically, when Jackson saw Morton's tombstone some five years later and read the inscription, he became so violent and angry that his friends had to hospitalize him. Charles Jackson remained in an insane asylum until he died seven years later on August 28, 1880.

William Morton had been fortunate in his experiments. Ether was a dangerous way to decrease pain because it could easily kill a patient. Before long, scientists discovered better anesthetics. In 1847, Scottish doctor James Simpson discovered that chloroform, a clear, heavy, sweet-smelling liquid, worked better than ether. In the 1860s, the gas nitrous oxide began to become popular and is still used widely today. The 1860s also saw the rise of cocaine as a painkiller that affected a small area of the body, called a local anesthetic. In 1904, novocaine, a synthesized substitute for cocaine, was introduced. During the twentieth century, the medical profession abandoned ether in favor of drugs such as Ethrane and Forane that work better and are much safer than ether.

Before the discovery of anesthetics, doctors and patients considered surgery as a last resort. People waited until it was a life-or-death situation before agreeing to suffer the agony of being cut open. After Morton introduced the world to anesthetics, surgery became commonplace. Surgeons could take their time and do operations properly, and patients were spared the terrible pain of surgery.

Queen Victoria of England (1819-1901) chose to use chloroform anesthetic while giving birth to her son Prince Leopold in 1853. She made the practice of using anesthetics during childbirth both popular and socially acceptable.

CHAPTER FIVE

Wilhelm Roentgen and X Rays

A scientist never knows when a great discovery will occur, and the best scientists are always on the lookout for things they cannot explain. If something mysterious happens in a laboratory, they do not rest until they find out why it happened. On November 8, 1895, a scientist named Wilhelm Roentgen (REN-ken) saw something that he could not explain. One of his experiments was glowing softly. The glow was barely noticeable and could easily have been missed, but Roentgen saw it. Curious, he wanted to know what had caused the glow. Little did he know that he was about to discover one of the most useful medical technologies of all time and would become a famous scientist as a result of his work. He had just discovered X rays.

Wilhelm Conrad Roentgen was born in Lennep, a small town in Germany, on March 27, 1845. When he was three years old, he moved with his parents to Apeldoorn, Holland. His parents,

A British reporter described Wilhelm Conrad Roentgen (1845-1923) as "clearly a man who, once upon the track of a mystery which appealed to him, would pursue it with unremitting vigour."

Charlotte and Friedrich, owned a small textile mill. Making a good living, they filled their home with Dutch paintings and fine china from Asia. Wilhelm was an only child, educated at private schools, and his parents had high hopes for him.

A bright, happy child, Wilhelm enjoyed roaming through the large forests that surrounded Apeldoorn. In the winter, he would skate on the frozen canals near his home. Throughout his life, he continued to spend his vacations at places where he could go on long nature walks.

Wilhelm's future seemed promising until the school he attended expelled him when he was 18 years old. The episode started when a fellow student drew a caricature of the teacher on the blackboard in front of the classroom. Since the teacher was not there, all of the students gathered at the blackboard to laugh at the picture. Wilhelm thought the picture so funny that he failed to notice when the teacher walked into the room and the others students sat down. When the teacher demanded that Wilhelm tell him who drew the picture, Wilhelm refused, so the school authorities asked him to leave the school. (Roentgen later told this story about himself, but the school claimed there were no records to substantiate the event.)

Wilhelm's father then hired a private tutor to teach his son at home. For the next year, Wilhelm studied science (which he liked) and Latin and Greek (which he did not like) in preparation for the college admissions examination. When the test day came, he was dismayed to find that the examiner was one of the teachers who had expelled him. Wilhelm failed the test. For the rest of his life, even when he became a teacher, Wilhelm hated exams.

The young Roentgen now decided to try to enter a university without having graduated from high school. The University of Utrecht allowed him to attend as a special student. There, he met another student who told him about a university in Zurich, Switzerland, that he could attend if he passed their entrance test. But the director of the Polytechnikum in Zurich was so impressed by Roentgen's work in school and his letter of application that he admitted him without the examination. At the age of 20, Roentgen was finally given a chance to show what he could do academically.

At the Polytechnikum, Roentgen studied engineering. Although he worked hard, he also liked to have fun. One of his favorite pastimes was renting a two-horse carriage and riding around in the city. He also liked to go with his friends to the Wirtschaft zum grunen Glas, the Green Glass Inn.

Johann Gottfried Ludwig, the owner of the establishment, was an unusual man. Ludwig had been studying to be a professor when his suspected revolutionary activities forced him to leave his home in Germany and flee to Switzerland. Unable to find a position at a university there, he bought the Green Glass Inn.

Many students who became acquainted with Ludwig would come to him for tutoring, especially in Latin. (The universities required students to write some of their papers in Latin.) He even taught many students how to fence, which was a popular university sport at the time. Scars on the cheek from swords were considered a sign of scholarship.

Roentgen did not care for fencing, but he did like to talk and argue with Ludwig. They became good friends and would often argue about politics and philosophy late into the night.

Ludwig had four grown children who helped him in the restaurant. One of his daughters, Anna Bertha, used to join in the discussions with her father and Roentgen. Soon Wilhelm Roentgen and Bertha Ludwig became close. They enjoyed taking nature walks and sailing.

Roentgen graduated from the university on August 6, 1868, with a degree in mechanical engineering. Even though he now had his degree, he did not know how he wanted to spend the rest of his life. Looking for advice, he went to one of his teachers, a physics professor named August Kundt, who suggested that Roentgen study physics. The young man took the professor's advice and continued his studies at the university. Less than a year later, on June 22, 1869, he obtained his Ph.D. degree in physics.

Following his graduation, Roentgen assisted Kundt with his classes and in the laboratory. During the next several years, Kundt moved to many different universities. Each time he accepted a new position, Roentgen followed him and continued to be his assistant. In 1872, Wilhelm and Bertha married.

Roentgen worked hard and earned the respect of his fellow scientists. In 1888, officials at the University of Würzburg asked him to come to

Germany and teach physics. There he was both a gifted scientist and a demanding teacher. He disliked lecturing and often mumbled during his classes, but he was humorous and always gave dramatic demonstrations of electricity, gasses, or whatever he was teaching. Although Roentgen was slightly colorblind, his vision was three times as sharp as normal. Sometimes his assistants would grow frustrated when they could not be as precise as Roentgen wanted them to be, simply because they could not see as well as he could.

Roentgen had many interests during this time and studied electricity, liquids, gasses, and light. It was experimenting with electricity that led him to his discovery of X rays in 1895.

This photograph of Wilhelm (standing) and Bertha (seated at right) was taken around 1889.

THE BREAKTHROUGH

In 1855, Heinrich Geissler, a glassblower in Germany, invented a pump that would remove all of the air from a glass tube. While the idea was not new, Geissler's device worked much better than any previous air-removing device. Working with Julius Plücker, a physics professor, Geissler filled the empty tubes with different gasses. Using an induction coil that produced high voltage, the two men discharged electricity into the tubes, which lit up in different colors depending on the type of gas they had put in the tubes.

While their experiments were pretty to look at, they did not seem useful. But Geissler and Plücker noticed something interesting. Faint rays of light came out of the cathode end of the glass tube, which released a beam of electrons into the gas. These rays came to be known as cathode rays.

Many scientists began experimenting with cathode rays. One of them, University of Münster professor Johann Hittorf, discovered that the rays could escape the tubes through tiny aluminum windows built into the glass. This made the rays more visible and, therefore, easier to study. Another German scientist, Philipp Lenard, also used aluminum to study rays. In addition, he covered the glass tubes with cardboard so only the cathode rays, and not the visible light, would escape. Lenard discovered that the cathode rays traveled only a few centimeters in the air before being absorbed by the air.

cathode: the electrode through which current passes from the nonmetallic to the metallic conductor; the negatively charged electrode

cathode rays: a stream of electrons emitted by the cathode in electrical discharge tubes

anode: the electrode through which current passes from the metallic to the nonmetallic conductor; the positively charged electrode

electrode: a terminal (usually a wire, rod, or plate) through which electric current passes between metallic and nonmetallic parts of an electric circuit

In June 1895, Wilhelm Roentgen began his own experiments with cathode rays. To begin, he repeated Lenard's experiments and used the same equipment: a Lenard tube (similar in size and shape to a long, thin test tube), a fluorescent screen, and a photographic plate.

That autumn, Roentgen continued experimenting. He was particularly interested in the faint glow of the cathode rays. Using a large Crookes tube (which looked like a large light bulb) without an aluminum window, he connected the tube to an induction coil, and then covered it in black cardboard so no visible light could escape.

Late in the afternoon of November 8, he darkened the room and waited a minute for his eyes to adjust. Then he turned on the electricity to test the ability of the black cardboard to block light. No light penetrated the cover, so he began to stop the current to set up his screen painted with barium platinocyanide, a metal that glows when exposed to cathode rays. Now he noticed a faint green light glowing from a bench about three feet from the tube. This was totally unexpected because all previous work with cathode rays indicated that the rays could travel no farther than an inch or two.

The result of the experiment excited Roentgen. To make sure that his eyes were not playing tricks on him, he tried it again. Then he lit a match and saw that the source of the brighter green light was the barium platinocyanide screen lying on the table. The screen had lit up, even though Roentgen had removed the aluminum window through which the

Crookes tubes are named for Sir William Crookes (1832-1919), who had performed many experiments with them during the 1870s. Crookes often complained to the manufacturer of his photographic materials that the plates the company sent him were fogged and useless, indicating that accidental X rays may have been made before Roentgen's discovery.

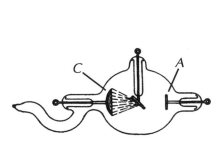

A Crookes tube used by Roentgen and other scientists. Electrons stream from the cathode (C) and hit the anode (A), transforming into invisible X rays that pass through the glass.

Dr. Otto Glasser, Roentgen's foremost biographer, described the discovery of X rays this way: "Suddenly, about a yard from the tube, Roentgen saw a weak light that shimmered on a little bench he knew was located nearby. It was as though a ray of light or a faint spark from the induction coil had been reflected by a mirror. Not believing this possible, he passed another series of discharges through the tube, and again the same fluorescence appeared. . . . Highly excited, Roentgen lit a match and to his great surprise discovered that the source of the mysterious light was the little barium platinocyanide screen lying on the bench."

cathode rays had escaped from the tube in Lenard's experiment. If cathode rays could not be causing the screen to glow, then something else had to be the source of the mysterious light.

Repeatedly, Roentgen tried the experiment, working late into the night. Each time, the screen began to glow softly, no matter how far away it was. Throughout the weekend, he repeated the experiment again and again. He would come upstairs from his laboratory, eat only a little, and then go back downstairs again without saying a word. His wife began to worry about him. Over the next few weeks, he stopped coming up for meals, and Bertha had to bring him his food on a tray. He set up a cot in his laboratory so he could take short naps and then stay up all night experimenting.

"When at first I made the startling discovery of the penetrating rays, it was such an extraordinarily astonishing phenomenon that I had to convince myself repeatedly by doing the same experiment over and over and over again to make absolutely certain that the rays actually existed," said Roentgen about this period of his life. "I was not aware of anything else. Any interference could have caused me to fail in the creation of identical conditions to substantiate the discovery."

In one test, Roentgen placed objects between the tube and the barium platinocyanide screen. First, he put a piece of paper between them. The screen still glowed brightly. Next, he tried a thick book and the screen dimmed only a little. Then he tried a piece of aluminum. The screen still glowed.

Then Roentgen held a sheet of lead between the tube and the screen. To his amazement, the lead stopped all of the rays. On the screen, he could see a dark shadow where he was holding the lead. Around the shadow was the same soft green glow. Roentgen thought he saw something else on the screen, right next to the shadow of the lead. He took a closer look and was amazed to see an outline of the bones in his hand on the screen!

Roentgen feared that no one would listen when he told them he could see people's bones with a strange new ray, and he thought that other scientists would accuse him of making up his story. Roentgen, therefore, decided that before he told anyone about his experiments, he would need absolute proof that these strange rays really existed.

Remembering that Philipp Lenard had shown how cathode rays affected photographic film, Roentgen decided to see if these new rays would also change the film. He took a photographic plate, put a piece of platinum on it, and then exposed it to the rays. Sure enough, the rays made the film dark, except in the areas covered by the platinum. Here the film was lighter in color because the platinum had absorbed the rays. He also made pictures of a compass and a shotgun. Finally, on December 22, he asked his wife, Bertha, to come with him to his lab.

Once in the lab, Wilhelm told Bertha about his experiments. He explained that placing her hand on the photographic plate for 15 minutes would not hurt her, so she agreed to let him take a picture of her hand. When her husband later showed her the

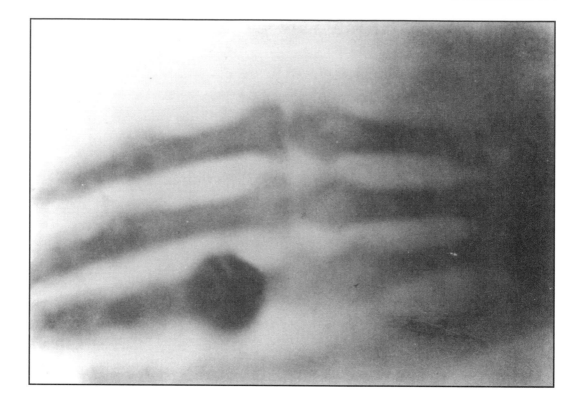

The famous X-ray photograph of Bertha Roentgen's hand that was made by her husband on December 22, 1895. The dark bulge on the fourth finger was her ring.

picture of the bones in her hand, she became very upset. She felt that looking at her own bones was like seeing herself already dead.

Roentgen now had the proof he needed. He collected all of his data and made several more pictures. Then he wrote a paper entitled "A New Kind of Ray" and sent it and copies of some of his pictures to a number of respected scientists. In the paper, he called the rays "X rays" because they were so mysterious. Roentgen had no idea that he was about to become world famous for his discovery.

THE RESULT

A scientific journal published "A New Kind of Ray," and the discovery was also reported in the news-papers. Soon Roentgen began to hear from people all over the world. Many sent letters congratulating him on his wonderful discovery. A few, however, were angry with him for creating "death rays which would surely destroy all mankind."

At first, no one was quite sure how to use this new discovery. Some religious groups thought that X-ray pictures showed proof of a human soul because they look so ghostly. Many people feared

This photograph of Wilhelm Roentgen was taken in 1906 at the Physical Institute of the Ludwig Maximilian University in Munich, Germany.

On February 3, 1896, a medical doctor named G. D. Frost brought a young patient of his to the Dartmouth College laboratory where his brother, Edwin Brant Frost, had been experimenting with the new Roentgen rays. The boy, Eddie McCarthy of Hanover, New Hampshire, had broken his forearm several weeks earlier. "No one could ever forget the interest felt in watching the development of the first plates," Edwin Frost later recalled. The image revealed "the fracture of the ulna very distinctly." This was the first diagnostic X ray made in North America.

for their privacy because X rays could see through walls and clothing. One company in London even started selling X-ray-proof underwear!

Before long, however, people began to realize the medical potential of X rays. For the first time, doctors would be able to see exactly where and how badly bones had been broken. X rays would make surgery easier because doctors could locate where an object, such as a bullet, had lodged before cutting into the patient.

Roentgen's discovery of X rays made possible the development of the fluoroscope. One disadvantage of X rays was that developing an X-ray picture took a long time. But by placing a fluorescent screen behind a patient, a fluoroscope allowed doctors to see the X-ray image instantly and know immediately what was going on inside a patient. The disadvantage was that, unlike an X-ray photograph, the fluoroscope did not make a permanent picture that doctors could keep to show other doctors or to compare to later X rays. The fluoroscope was discovered in 1896 almost simultaneously by Princeton physics professor William Francis Magie on February 8, and by three Italian scientists—Angelo Bateli and Antonio Garbasso sometime in January and Enrico Salvioni on February 5.

Not much time passed before people realized that X rays had a negative side: they were a type of radiation. Too much exposure to X rays could burn the skin, like a bad sunburn, and patients exposed too long to X rays would lose their hair. Among those who were injured by X rays was the American inventor Thomas Edison, who improved the fluoroscope and designed a complete X-ray unit. While doing this work, he was often exposed to the rays and, as a result, was badly burned. In fact, in the first 60 years of X-ray technology, 359 people died of overexposure to the rays. (Roentgen had always stood behind a lead screen when working with X rays, a precaution he had probably taken so that he could define his X-ray beam and prevent his photographic plates from fogging.)

While some doctors and scientists investigated the uses of X rays, others tried to explain what the rays were. By 1897, Joseph Thomson in England came to the conclusion that X rays are a type of electromagnetic radiation, which is an invisible form of light energy. His theory was later confirmed by other scientists. Ultraviolet rays are another type of

Thomas Edison looks at an assistant's hand through a fluoroscope at his laboratory in West Orange, New Jersey.

electromagnetic radiation, and so are radio waves. Because X rays are short in length and high in energy, they can penetrate solid objects.

In 1901, Roentgen received the first Nobel Prize awarded in the area of physics for his discovery of X rays. For the rest of his life, nations and universities all over the world honored him with numerous awards. Wilhelm Roentgen died on February 10, 1923. World War I and the death of Bertha in 1919 had made the last years of his life hard ones, but Roentgen never lost his spirit. He loved life and was always excited by new ideas.

Throughout the twentieth century, new and better technologies have been developed for looking inside the human body. One technique, called computed tomography, or CT, rotates tubes that beam X rays around a patient. The scanner uses X-ray detectors and a computer to produce cross-sectional images, or tomograms, of the body's interior. This gives doctors a clear view of soft tissues, such as brain matter or muscles, that look shadowy on a standard X-ray photograph.

Radiated energy is described in terms of its wavelengths and its frequency; that is, the distance between successive wave crests and the number of crests that arrive each second. The waves range from short, high-frequency gamma rays to the long, low-frequency radio waves on what is called the electromagnetic spectrum.

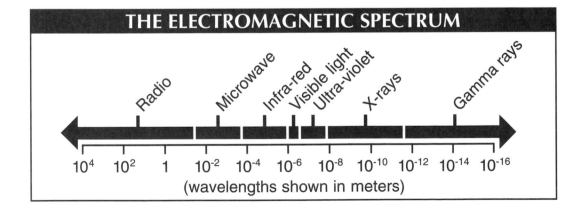

THE ELECTROMAGNETIC SPECTRUM

Radio Microwave Infra-red Visible light Ultra-violet X-rays Gamma rays

10^4 10^2 1 10^{-2} 10^{-4} 10^{-6} 10^{-8} 10^{-10} 10^{-12} 10^{-14} 10^{-16}

(wavelengths shown in meters)

Not all scans use X rays. One of the most common scans today is called magnetic resonance imaging, or MRI. MRIs use powerful magnets to make pictures that are more detailed than are possible to make with X rays. Ultrasonic scanners produce another kind of picture called a sonogram. Ultrasound waves, which are sound waves above the range of normal hearing, bounce off objects, causing echoes that are then converted into electronic signals to form an image. Doctors often use ultrasound to determine whether a baby is developing normally while still in the mother's womb.

In spite of the new innovations, however, X rays remain the most common way of seeing into the human body. This wonderful technology all began when Wilhelm Roentgen saw an unexpected green glow in a dark room.

Computed tomography (CT), a more sophisticated X-ray machine, can make a head-to-toe scan of this patient's body in seconds.

CHAPTER SIX

Marie Curie
and Radiation Therapy

Before long, another scientist discovered other powerful rays that, when used correctly, could destroy cancer cells in the body and give doctors a new treatment for the disease.

This scientist, Marie Curie, was born on November 7, 1867, in Warsaw, Poland. Her given name was Marya Sklodovski (also spelled Sklodowska), but everyone called her Manya. Her father, Vladislav, taught physics and mathematics, and her mother, Bronislawa, was a musician who also ran a boarding school. Manya was the youngest of five children.

Times were difficult in Poland then. The area that Manya lived in was controlled by Russia, and Polish children were forced to speak Russian in school. They were not allowed to learn about the history of their own country but had to learn Russian history instead. Men and women like the Sklodovskis who were not "pro-Russian" did not

Scientist Marie Curie (1867-1934) won two Nobel prizes for her pioneering work, one in chemistry and one in physics.

prosper. The Sklodovski family had to move many times, and each time they found themselves in a smaller apartment in a worse neighborhood. To earn money, the family took in boarders.

Sadly, by the time Manya was five years old, her mother had developed tuberculosis. To keep from infecting her children, she did not hug and kiss them, and she ate from separate dishes. Bronislawa was also separated from her family for a time while at a clinic, trying to recover her health.

When Manya was nine years old, two of her older sisters, Zosia and Bronya, caught typhus from one of the boarders, and Zosia died. Two years later, her mother died from tuberculosis, and Bronya had to run the household.

Manya could read by the time she was four, and she was a brilliant student. She spoke perfect Russian, and teachers often called on her when Russian inspectors came to see how things were going in the classroom. Young Manya had an amazing memory and an ability to concentrate despite distractions and noise. At home, her brother and sisters often teased her while she was studying by swooping around her, yelling, trying to break her concentration.

After Manya graduated from the gymnasium, the equivalent of today's high school, her father told her to take a year off as a reward for her hard work. She spent the year traveling the Polish countryside, visiting relatives.

Like many young Polish students, Manya believed that the only way her people could hope to free Poland from Russian rule was to become edu-cated. So she often attended secret classes where she learned about science, philosophy, and Polish history. When she was 17, Manya decided to earn money so that her sister Bronya could attend medical school in Paris. There were not many opportunities for young women in Poland, and this was Bronya's best chance to escape Russian rule.

After first refusing Manya's generous offer, Bronya finally accepted, but only after making her younger sister promise to follow her to Paris in a year or two. Manya agreed. She earned money by becoming a tutor and nanny for the children of the wealthy Zorawski family who lived in Szczuki, a town north of Warsaw. Although the Zorawskis were rich, many poor peasants lived in Szczuki. In her spare time, Manya taught the local children.

By 1890, Bronya had completed medical school and married a fellow student with whom she set up a practice in Paris. When Bronya asked her to come to Paris, Manya was reluctant to leave Poland, but she knew she had to be educated to help change her homeland. She saved her money and, in the autumn of 1891, left for Paris. Manya, now using the French version of her name, Marie, entered the University of Paris, determined to study science.

The freedom that people enjoyed in France astounded Marie. In Poland, the Russians did not allow people to speak their own language at school or at work. In Paris, however, people could speak whatever language they wanted, and they could also study whatever they wished. And people could talk

When she reached Paris, Marie Curie studied hard and enjoyed the freedom of her new home.

about politics without worrying about who would hear them and report them to the Russians.

At first, classes were hard for Marie. She did not speak French very well, and she lagged behind many of her classmates academically. She needed to do a considerable amount of work to catch up, but she would let nothing stand in her way. Her studies totally absorbed her. In fact, her sister Bronya worried that Marie was not living a very healthy life. Marie did not eat very much and lived on buttered bread, radishes, and tea. Her small apartment was usually cold.

At school, Marie was shy, and she did not talk to many people except when she was in her science classes. She was so intent on becoming one of the top science students at the university that by 1893 she had finished a master's degree in physics. Just one year later, she earned a master's degree in mathematics.

In the spring of 1894, the Society for the Encouragement of National Industry awarded Marie a grant to study the magnetic properties of various types of steel. One of her teachers introduced Marie to another scientist who was an expert in this field, 35-year-old Pierre Curie.

Like Marie, Pierre was shy and quiet. A brilliant scientist, he usually refused honors and awards because he hated to be in the spotlight. He did research because of his interest in science, not to receive recognition. When he realized that he and Marie had so much in common, Pierre became very attracted to the young Polish woman.

Pierre asked Marie to marry him, but she refused because she was not sure that she wanted to stay in France after she earned her Ph.D. degree. But Pierre was so in love that he offered to leave his homeland and live with Marie in Poland. He asked Bronya to talk to Marie for him, and, finally, he won her over. Marie realized that she was in love, and she and Pierre were married on July 26, 1895. Manya Sklodovski was now Marie Curie. The following day, the couple took off on new bicycles and spent their honeymoon exploring the French countryside.

In order to be awarded a Ph.D., the highest college degree, a student had to do a large research project. For her project, Marie chose to study a discovery made by the physicist Henri Becquerel. Her experiments would lead to her great discoveries about radioactivity.

Pierre Curie was already an established scientist when he met Marie Sklodovski in 1894.

THE BREAKTHROUGH

French physicist Henri Becquerel, excited by Roentgen's discovery of X rays in 1895, was experimenting with materials that glow in ultraviolet light, including uranium, an element that gives off rays that pass through matter, just like X rays.

Becquerel published a scientific article about the results of his experiments. Unfortunately, since his rays were not as powerful or as spectacular as X rays, no one in the scientific community paid much attention to his article. Becquerel experimented for a while longer, looking for ways to make the rays stronger. Eventually, he gave up trying and went back to testing other materials.

Becquerel's article, however, had caught the attention of Marie Curie, who wanted to find out what had caused the rays he wrote about. She chose this as her research topic, but her pregnancy and the birth of the Curies' first daughter, Irène, on September 12, 1897, temporarily interrupted her project. Pierre offered to help. Pierre and his brother Jacques had made a piezo-quartz electrometer when the two were studying piezo, or pressure, electricity. They used this instrument, which was much more sensitive and accurate than those Becquerel had used, to measure the rays.

One of Curie's teachers, Paul Schützenberger, who cofounded the School of Industrial Physics and Chemistry in Paris, allowed her to use a vacant storeroom for her laboratory. The room was large, but it was also damp and unheated, and the roof leaked.

Electricity can be produced directly from heat, pressure, or light. Pressure, or piezo, electricity is a phenomenon during which certain crystals produce an electric current when squeezed or stretched. The amount of electricity generated equals the amount of pressure applied, making this effect useful in measuring pressure as well as tiny electrical charges. Piezoelectricity was used in the first crystal radio sets during the First World War.

Marie and Pierre Curie shared all their daily tasks, from the work in their laboratory to caring for their young daughter, Irène.

element: in chemistry and physics, a material that cannot be broken down into other substances and which contains only one kind of atom. There are 109 known elements; 94 occur naturally, 15 are produced artificially.

mineral: a natural inorganic (not alive) substance. Rocks are combinations of minerals. A few minerals are elements (i.e., gold, silver, and iron) but most are chemical compounds or mixtures.

Sometimes, the temperature would drop to near freezing. These conditions were hard on the delicate equipment that the Curies were using, but they had to make do because there were no other laboratories available.

When Marie Curie began experimenting on uranium, she quickly discovered that the strange rays appeared whether the uranium was wet or dry, pure or impure, and whether the experiments were done in the light or in the dark. During her early experiments, she also discovered that another element—thorium—gave off rays similar to the ones emitted by uranium. Curie used the word "radioactive" to describe materials that give off rays.

In her study of radioactivity, Curie tested hundreds of mineral samples. As she examined sample after sample, measuring the amount of radioactivity in each one, Curie realized that some samples released stronger rays than could be accounted for based on the amounts of uranium or thorium the samples contained. This could only mean that there must be a new, highly radioactive element, one that had not yet been discovered.

Now Curie began to search for this new, undiscovered element. If she could purify it, she would be able to create a source of radioactivity that would be much more powerful than uranium. Realizing how important his wife's work was, Pierre set aside some of his own experiments so he could assist her.

In July 1898, the Curies had isolated a pinch of powder from pitchblende, a variety of the mineral called uraninite. This powder contained a new

Marie Curie and her daughter Irène (1897-1956), who would follow her mother's example and become a scientist herself. She also married a fellow scientist, Frédéric Joliot. The Joliot-Curies shared the Nobel Prize for chemistry in 1935.

element hundreds of times more radioactive than the uranium. They named the new element polonium, in honor of Poland, Marie's homeland.

As they broke pitchblende down into its elements, the Curies discovered that it had not one, but two radioactive elements. The scientists named the second element radium, from the Latin word *radius*, which means ray. Because radium appeared to be more radioactive than polonium, Marie and Pierre decided to try and purify this second element first. At the time, they were unaware that they would need 50 tons of water and six tons of chemicals to treat one ton of pitchblende and obtain five to six grams of radium.

Of course, the Curies did not have a ton of pitchblende sitting around. Fortunately, pitchblende is commonly found in the rocks leftover from mining operations, as it is a component in the ores of quartz and other metals that are mined. The Austrian government offered Marie Curie as much pitchblende as she wanted, free of charge, if she paid the shipping costs. They used their life savings to transport the material to France, and she and Pierre worked long hours with as much pitchblende as their largest cast-iron pot would hold. Since the process gave off toxic fumes, they had to work outside. The process was slow, and weeks ran into months. Finally, Pierre Curie convinced a local factory to help them by doing most of the processing of the pitchblende.

Five long years passed before Curie reached her goal. She had started her research project in 1898 and did not finish it until 1902. During those years, she and her husband discovered that the element radium was a pure source of radioactivity and two million times more radioactive than the element uranium.

Radium was a fascinating new element. It gave off heat, glowed in the dark, discolored glass, and could make other substances—even air—radioactive. Radium would later help scientists discover the structure of the atom. Before that revelation, however, the Curies and others would find that it could kill living cells—including cancer cells.

THE RESULT

Henri Becquerel was the first person to make the discovery that radium could kill skin cells. He was carrying around a sample of radium that the Curies had sent him when he noticed that near his pocket, his skin was red. He told the Curies about his finding, and Pierre, a true scientist, taped some radium against his skin in order to test Becquerel's observation. Only a couple of days passed before the radium left a large red burn on his skin. Months would pass before the wound healed.

Henri Becquerel (Beh-KREL) (1852-1908) was a member of a family of physicists. Both his father, A. E. Becquerel, and his grandfather were physicists who worked at the Museum of Natural History in Paris, as did Henri.

Once doctors and scientists recognized that radioactivity destroyed skin cells, they began wondering if it could also kill cancer cells. The first person to experiment with cancer cells was Henri Danlus, a French doctor. Pierre Curie also did some research. The two men came to the same conclusion: radiation kills both skin cells and cancer cells. The difference is that while skin cells grow back, cancer cells do not. This form of treatment for cancer was named Curietherapy in France, and it is now known as radiation therapy.

In 1903, Marie Curie became the first woman in France to receive a Ph.D. in science. Later that year, the Nobel committee awarded Marie Curie, Pierre Curie, and Henri Becquerel the Nobel Prize in physics for their research.

The Curies were becoming famous around the world. Newspaper reporters everywhere wrote about how the French couple spent years of their lives doing hard physical labor under primitive conditions and had not even been paid. The newspapers pointed out that because radium was so difficult to find, it became very expensive to buy, so the Curies would have become multimillionaires had they applied for a patent for their method of extracting this element. But Marie and Pierre believed their discovery belonged to the world.

The Curie family grew to four when Ève, their second daughter, was born on December 6, 1904. Ève was 16 months old when, on April 19, 1906, Pierre was crossing the street on a rainy day. Lost in thought, he was struck and killed by a horse-drawn carriage. Although her husband's death devastated Marie, she remembered something that Pierre had once told her: "Whatever happens, even if one should become like a body without a soul, still one must always work." Science was Marie Curie's life, so, although she would forever miss her best friend and husband, she returned to the laboratory. She also took over Pierre's teaching duties at the University of Paris. Curie won a second Nobel Prize in 1911, this time in chemistry, for discovering radium and polonium. In 1912, the Radium Institute was jointly constructed by the University and the Pasteur Institute. Marie Curie was named director.

During Curie's lifetime, scientists knew that radiation could kill skin and cancer cells, but they did not really understand all the harmful effects of radiation. Ever since she had begun working with uranium, Curie had been exposed to a steady stream of intense radiation. She knew that lead blocked radiation, but she rarely bothered to protect herself. The many years of working with radioactive materials caused her to tire easily and often feel ill. Her early experiments left her fingertips raw and tender for the rest of her life.

Despite her health problems, Curie helped her country when World War I erupted in Europe in 1914. Knowing that X-ray machines were by far the best way to find the shrapnel, or shell fragments, in a soldier's wound, Curie was influential in organizing a program that equipped small trucks with the machines. Using these mobile X-ray machines, doctors could travel to wherever they were needed

One of the many mobile X-ray machines used during World War I. More than 1 million soldiers were X rayed during the war.

to X ray the wounded soldiers. Along with her teenage daughter, Irène, Curie helped doctors working on the battlefields.

After the war, Curie returned to teaching and to her work as director of the Radium Institute. The war had left the laboratory short of funds and equipment. When this became known to the public, Curie was invited to travel to the United States. During Curie's 1921 visit, President Warren G. Harding presented her with a gram of radium for the Institute—worth $100,000 at the time.

On July 4, 1934, Marie Curie died of leukemia, a type of cancer, at age 67. Radiation from radium, which saved many lives by killing cancer cells, also caused cancer. Her coffin was placed above Pierre's, and her sister Bronya and her brother Jozef each threw a handful of Polish dirt on top of it. All the world mourned the loss of the great scientist.

Throughout the twentieth century, scientists have refined and improved radiation therapy. Today, doctors use many different types of radiation to destroy cancer cells. An advantage of radiation therapy is that it is less invasive than surgery. For example, without radiation therapy, doctors might choose to remove the voice box of a patient with laryngeal cancer, and he or she would probably never speak again. Instead, radiation therapy has offered hope to many cancer patients.

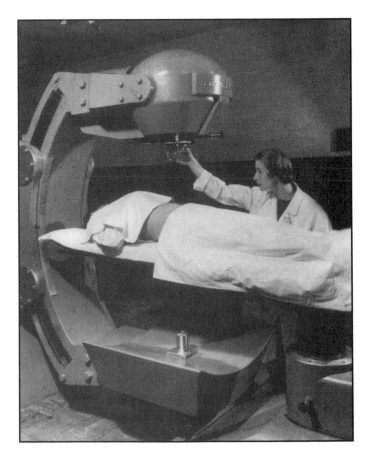

A patient receives radiation treatment for cancer from this cobalt-teletherapy machine. The radiation prevents cancer cells from dividing and destroys them. The radiation can also kill healthy cells, causing some patients to experience hair loss or nausea.

CHAPTER SEVEN

Willem Einthoven and the Electrocardiograph

Today, electricity powers light bulbs and televisions. Yet, more than two thousand years before these inventions, people recognized the phenomenon of electricity, although they had no name for or understanding of it. Thales (624-526 B.C.), a Greek scientist, studied magnets and what is today called static electricity. Two centuries later, the Greek philosopher Aristotle (384-322 B.C.) wrote that a sea creature, the torpedo ray, "narcotizes" its prey with a "shock." People later learned that, although invisible, electricity actually flows through objects and all animals—including humans. In fact, the human heart beats because of electrical impulses in the muscle cells of the heart.

In the 1890s, Willem Einthoven (EYENT-hoh-fen) invented a way to measure heartbeats. He called his invention the electrocardiograph. This has since been shortened to ECG or EKG, from the German word, *Elektrokardiogramme*. Today, these

Willem Einthoven (1860-1927) not only invented the electrocardiograph machine but also helped to interpret the readings it made.

The Greek scientist Thales (THAY-leez) discovered that when he rubbed amber (the gum or resin from trees that has fossilized and turned solid), it attracted tiny bits of any lightweight objects, such as thread or feathers. Many years later, Englishman Walter Charleton called this power of attraction electricity, from the Greek word *elektron,* which means amber.

machines are commonly used in hospitals by doctors to check whether a patient's heart is beating regularly. The first ECGs, however, looked very different from those found in modern hospitals.

Willem Einthoven was born on May 21, 1860, in Semarang, Java, in the Dutch East Indies (now Indonesia), where his father, Jacob, was the town's doctor. Jacob Einthoven died when Willem was only six years old. Four years later, his mother, Louise, brought Willem and his five younger brothers and sisters back to Europe so they could receive a better education.

At home in Utrecht, in the Netherlands, Willem went to a new kind of high school. At that time, most high school students studied Latin and Greek. This new school, however, dropped those languages and taught more science instead. But Willem found out that he could not earn an advanced degree unless he knew Latin, so he studied this ancient language on his own.

By the time Willem was 18, he had decided that he wanted to follow in his father's footsteps and become a doctor in the Dutch military. He discovered that the Dutch government would pay for medical school if he promised to join the army after he graduated. So Willem Einthoven enrolled in medical school at the University of Utrecht.

Eager to learn, Einthoven excelled in his classwork and was also active in sports. He was a championship fencer and enjoyed rowing and gymnastics as well. In fact, a gymnastics accident provided the subject for Einthoven's first scientific paper. When he broke his wrist, he took the opportunity to study how the human arm twists and moves. In 1882, a scientific journal published his paper, "Some Remarks on the Elbow Joint."

While at medical school, Einthoven became interested in ophthalmology, the study of the eyes. He was inspired by a teacher named Frans Cornelis Donders, who had been one of the most famous opthalmologists in Europe before becoming a

Franciscus Cornelis Donders (1818-1889) discovered the causes of two common vision problems, farsightedness and astigmatism. Because of his findings, ophthalmologists were able to make more accurate eyeglass lenses to compensate for these conditions.

professor at the University of Utrecht in 1863. Einthoven's graduation dissertation on how the eye perceives different colors was given a cum laude (with honor) award and later published.

Although Einthoven had planned on serving as a military doctor in the East Indies after graduating in 1885, an offer of a professorship from the University of Leiden changed his mind. At Leiden, he would be able to teach and do research. Donders had recommended his student for this position because of Einthoven's excellent research skills.

For not fulfilling his military obligations, Einthoven would have to pay back to the Dutch government all the money he had been given for medical school. And because he would have to do this on a professor's salary, he knew he would be in debt for a long time. Still, Einthoven decided that the offer to teach at Leiden was too good to pass up. He became a professor of physiology, which is the study of the function of living organisms and their parts.

Two months after becoming a professor at Leiden University, Einthoven married his cousin, Frederique Jeanne Louise de Vogel. They had three daughters and one son. Their son, Willem Frederick, grew up to become an electrical engineer who sometimes helped his father with his experiments. One daughter, Johanna, became a physician.

At Leiden, Einthoven quickly gained a reputation for being a kind and modest person. He rode to the university on his bicycle. When he arrived, the first thing he would do was to put on comfortable slippers. He spoke Dutch, German, French, and English and made friends all over the world. Einthoven loved to tell people about his work. He was also known as a great scientist who did his experiments carefully and never jumped to conclusions. "The truth is all that matters," Einthoven said. "What you or I think is inconsequential."

Along with studying human vision, Einthoven was also interested in respiration, or how people breathe. He spent a considerable amount of time studying asthma, which makes breathing difficult for some people, and proved that asthma was caused by spasms of the muscles in the bronchi. (The bronchi are the tubes the allow air into the lungs.) He published his results in 1892 and gained wide recognition for the importance of this study.

Einthoven's wife's brother, Willem de Vogel, was also studying medicine. While in medical school in 1891, Vogel began to study with Einthoven. Every medical student was required to construct an experiment and write about it before graduating. When Vogel asked Einthoven for ideas, Einthoven suggested that he study electrical activity in the heart. Both men liked the idea, so they began working together.

When Aristotle and others had observed that some fish emitted, or gave off, electric currents, they thought this occurred because of something unique to those particular fish. In 1787, a scientist named Luigi Galvani (gahl-VAH-nee) discovered that all animals have electricity running through them. At the time, he was experimenting on a frog in a lab at the University of Bologna in Italy. The frog was still alive but partially dissected. While Galvani was using a nearby machine that gave off static electricity, a lab assistant accidentally left a metal knife touching a nerve on one of the frog's leg muscles.

Galvani was surprised to find that whenever he used the machine, the legs on the frog would jump. He realized that the metal knife was conducting electricity to the nerve, which signaled the muscles to move. After more experimentation, he discovered that nerves send electric signals throughout the body at all times. Whenever a muscle moves, it is because the brain has sent a tiny electrical signal through the nerves to the muscles.

Later, galvanometer machines designed to measure electricity in the body were named after Luigi Galvani. The first galvanometers were made about 1825. Because they measured electricity directly from exposed muscles, a scientist had to cut open an animal in order to measure the amount of electric current.

Then, in the mid-1880s, Augustus Waller took the next big step in measuring electricity in an animal's body. Waller discovered that every time a heart beats, electricity can also be detected on the skin. In 1887, Waller demonstrated his finding for other scientists. He put his right hand and his left foot into buckets filled with saltwater and hooked up a galvanometer to the buckets. Saltwater conducts electricity, so every time his heart beat, the mercury in a tube in the galvanometer would rise. He also did the experiment on his bulldog, Jimmy.

Italian anatomist Luigi Galvani (1737-1798) lent his name to many electrical items besides the galvanometer, including galvanic electricity (the steady electricity created by two metals in contact) and galvanized iron (iron on which crystals of zinc are layered using an electric current). A person moved to sudden action is "galvanized."

Waller had found a safe way to measure the electrical current inside the heart. He did not think, however, that his discovery could be used as a medical device. His galvanometer was not very sensitive, and it took a long time to make good readings.

Willem Einthoven poses with his string galvanometer at the Physiological Laboratory in Leiden, Holland, in June 1920.

THE BREAKTHROUGH

Einthoven wanted to develop a machine that worked more accurately than Waller's. In 1900, he began to build what he called a string galvanometer. Instead of using mercury in a tube, Einthoven's galvanometer consisted of a thin fiber of quartz coated with silver because he thought this thin piece of fiber would be much more responsive than the mercury-filled tube used by Waller. Einthoven suspended the fiber between two poles of an electromagnet, which created a steady magnetic field. Einthoven knew that if a current of electricity went through it, the fiber would become magnetic. The poles of the electromagnet would either repel or attract the magnetic fiber, causing it to move back and forth.

Einthoven believed that if he attached the string galvanometer to a person's skin, every heartbeat would create enough energy to move the fiber. Because the fiber was so thin, the electricity made by the heart would be enough to make the fiber magnetic. He planned to make a record with the tip of the fiber as it moved. This graph, made by a pen on a moving strip of paper, would show the doctor a patient's heartbeat. A doctor could easily learn how to examine the graph, which Einthoven named the electrocardiogram, and then determine if a patient's heart was beating normally. If not, the doctor could tell what was wrong by the shape of the line.

As he experimented, Einthoven ran into many problems. The only way to get the fiber thin enough was to attach one end of a heated quartz wire to an

electromagnet: a piece of soft iron that becomes a magnet when a coil of insulated wire is wrapped around it and an electric current flows through the wire

electrocardiograph: an instrument that makes a record of the electric activity of the heart

electrocardiogram: the recording made by an electrocardiograph

arrow and shoot it across the room, stretching the wire thinner. Moreover, the electromagnet he made was so large and so strong that Einthoven had to cool it with water to keep the magnet from overheating.

The completed string galvanometer weighed 600 pounds, and five people were needed to operate it. But the machine worked. Metal sensors stuck on a person's skin sent electrical signals to the string galvanometer quickly and accurately, and the ECGs were very detailed.

A normal heartbeat shows a pattern of regularly occurring spikes and dips that Einthoven named P, Q, R, S, and T waves. By studying the pattern and frequency of these waves, doctors could determine whether a patient's heart was beating normally.

Wave patterns of a healthy heart as recorded on an electrocardiogram.
P wave: the heart is excited by small electric charges in the heart's cells.
Q-R-S wave complex: the "beat," a high speed wave resulting from the heart's contraction.
T wave: a mild wave that washes over the heart as it relaxes, ready for the next P wave.
This entire process takes less than one second.

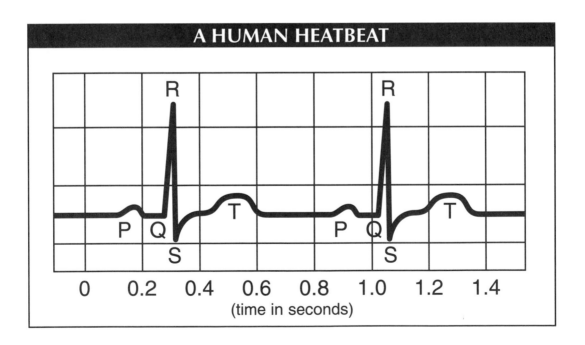

A HUMAN HEATBEAT

THE RESULT

Because the string galvanometer was so huge, it could not be moved from Einthoven's lab to the hospital. Instead, Einthoven had telephone wires strung from his lab to the hospital, which was about one mile away. Over these wires, Einthoven could monitor the heartbeats of patients in the hospital. In fact, doctors became frustrated when Einthoven could sometimes make a diagnosis faster than they could, even though he was not even in the same room as the patient. These early ECGs were called telecardiograms.

In 1903, Einthoven unveiled the string galvanometer to the world. Soon afterward, he reached an agreement for the Edelmann and Sons firm in Munich to manufacture string galvanometers, later renamed electrocardiographs.

Following a dispute over royalties with the company, Einthoven worked with the Cambridge Scientific Instrument Company to make electrocardiograph equipment in England and the United States. This company was founded by Horace Darwin, the youngest son of the great biologist Charles Darwin. The first Cambridge electrocardiograph was manufactured in 1912.

Einthoven continued to refine his invention and research how to interpret the machine's readings. In 1924, Einthoven visited the United States, where he gave lectures at numerous schools and toured hospitals and laboratories. While reading a newspaper one day, he came upon an article that reported he had been awarded the Nobel Prize in medicine and physiology! The world now recognized Willem Einthoven as the "Father of Electrocardiography." Three years later, Einthoven developed cancer. He died on September 28, 1927, at the age of 67.

ECGs are still common in hospitals today. One of the greatest advantages of the electrocardiograph is that it creates a permanent record of the heartbeat. Physicians can compare this record to ECGs taken at different times or show them to other doctors to ask their opinions. Before the ECG, recording how the heartbeat changed over time was difficult, and doctors could not ask the opinion of other medical experts unless the patient was present for examination.

Scientists have progressed from using electricity to monitor the heart and now use it to help the heart function. When someone has heart disease or has had a heart attack, the heart often beats irregularly. The pacemaker, invented by American engineer Wilson Greatbatch in 1953, provides the heart with a steady source of electricity. Powered by a tiny battery, the pacemaker releases small amounts of electricity that tell the heart when to contract, or beat. Today, some people with pacemakers can call their physicians and have their implants checked over the telephone.

As technology advances, scientists are developing more ways to monitor, control, and even replace the human heart. In 1953, the heart-lung machine came into use. This machine performs the work of these two vital organs for short periods of

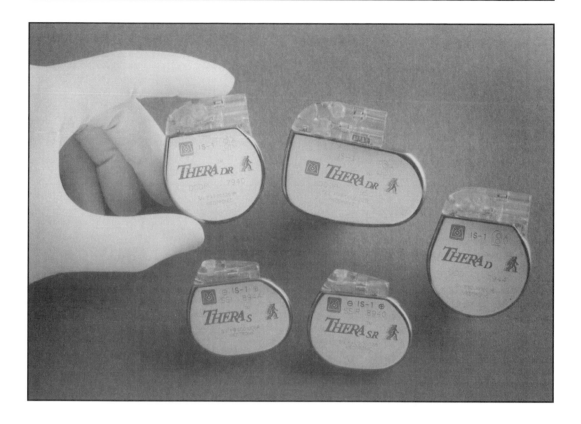

time so surgeons can operate on a person's heart or lungs. It also made possible the first human heart transplant on December 3, 1967, by South African surgeon Christiaan Barnard.

The first artificial heart was implanted in a patient in 1982. Although not yet perfected, artificial hearts are sometimes used to keep a patient alive until a donated human heart becomes available for transplant.

Today's pacemakers are designed to pace, or regulate, the contraction of the chambers of the heart. They can be programmed to a fixed rate or adjusted to the body's circulatory needs.

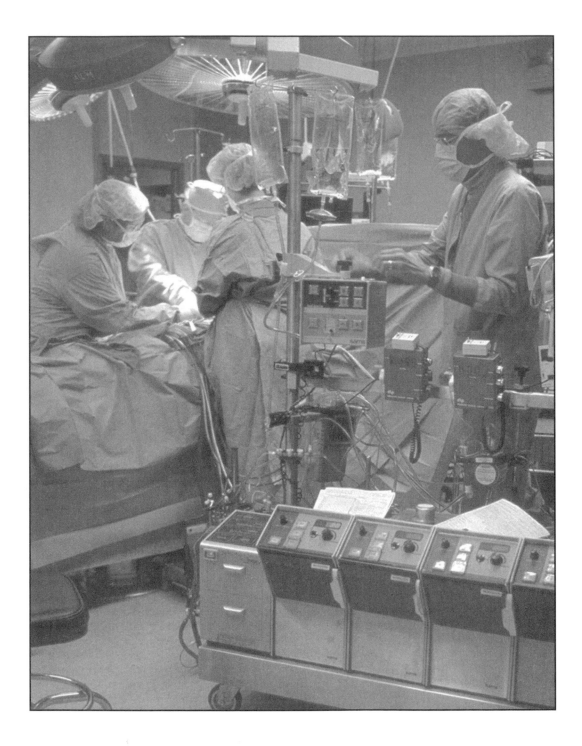

Looking Forward to Better Health

With innovations like X rays and anesthetics, medicine changed radically in the nineteenth century. The introduction of antibiotics in the 1940s gave doctors a new power to cure diseases and infections that they previously could only identify.

Then in the late twentieth century, the computer began a new technological medical revolution. Now doctors working with computers are changing the medical world, from recordkeeping to diagnosis. Some hospitals are currently computerizing all of their patient records and eliminating as much paperwork as possible. The computer, for example, can sort through and combine thousands of case histories, making it easier for medical professionals to recognize trends or gather information about different treatments in order to evaluate how well they are working.

Computers are having an especially large impact in the field of surgery. Surgeons usually have

In today's operating room, surgery and other medical procedures have advanced rapidly with the use of computers.

to cut into the human body to remove or repair damaged parts. Using machines for X-ray computed tomography and magnetic resonance imaging, doctors can now use computers to create images of the inside of the human body. As medical machines become more powerful, doctors will be able to use them for image-guided therapy. Soon they will be able to strap on a pair of goggles and explore the inside of a person's body without cutting the patient open. And that's just the beginning. Once doctors have perfected such virtual exploratory surgery, they will be able to operate without having to make a single incision in the body.

A physician in the future, for example, might be able to explore a tumor without actually cutting the patient's skin. Then, using virtual images, the doctor could destroy the tumor by aiming ultrasound waves (powerful sound waves much higher-pitched than humans can hear) at it. The surgeon performing the operation will not have to be in the same room, or even the same country, as the patient. Using satellites, a doctor will be able to perform surgery on a patient anywhere in the world without having to leave his or her office.

In fact, operations in the future may not need human surgeons at all. Instead, robots could do the work. The first surgical robot was made in 1989. Its first operation was removing a patient's prostate (the male gland that helps to produce semen). The robot successfully performed this delicate procedure in 20 minutes, one that would take a human surgeon three times as long to perform. In 1995, doctors were conducting clinical trials of a robot that performs hip replacements. The robot can hollow out a cavity in the thighbone where the prosthesis, or artificial hip joint, can be placed with greater accuracy than by a human surgeon. One day, scientists may develop tiny robots that a patient can swallow or a doctor can inject into the patient. Once in the body, these robots would seek out a diseased part of the body and then make the needed repairs.

It is also possible that much less surgery may be needed in the future because genetic engineering will have corrected many of the health problems that require surgery today. Genetic engineering—the ability to clone, or reproduce another gene exactly, or splice together genetic information—has been in use since the early 1970s and will continue to make advances. Human insulin, for example, is now genetically engineered, by taking a cloned gene coding for human insulin and transferring it to bacteria where it reproduces.

Many diseases are the result of genetic flaws, a mistake in a person's DNA (deoxyribonucleic acid), which is the blueprint from which living things are created. By looking for flaws in DNA, scientists might one day be able to predict at birth what diseases people will be prone to developing and then recommend preventative measures. In 1993, they found the gene that carries Huntington's disease, and the discovery of a gene that causes breast cancer soon followed.

The solution, then, is not only to find out what diseases a person may develop but also to correct

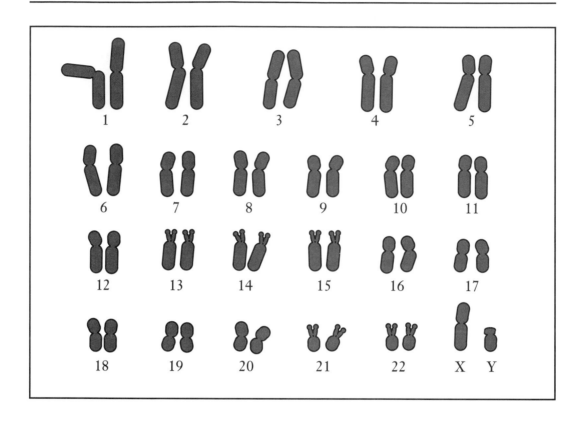

The 23 pairs of human chromosomes carry all the genetic information needed to create a new person. Geneticists are "mapping" these chromosomes, learning which chromosome carries specific genes and exactly where on the chromosome that gene is located.

the genetic flaw. In 1990, doctors altered the genes of a four-year-old girl. She had a rare disease called severe combined immunodeficiency (SCID). This disease cripples a body's immune system so it cannot defend itself from diseases. In the past, people with SCID have had to live their lives in plastic bubbles to keep them safe from disease. By genetically altering the genes of this child, however, doctors were able to restore her immune system.

Soon, doctors may be able to correct the DNA of people who have not yet developed a disease, and, in effect, cure patients of diseases they have not even contracted yet! Scientists may also be able to alter people's DNA to allow them to live longer.

There is much debate about where the line should be drawn in genetic engineering. If doctors can alter DNA to stop people from developing certain diseases, they can also alter people in other ways. A person could be made taller or shorter, or more intelligent. Who should have the power to make these decisions? How do we guard against misuse of this new knowledge?

But others are more optimistic about the current medical revolution and DNA research. Computers will help surgeons perform surgery without cutting the skin, aid diagnosis, and streamline the whole medical information process. By the year 2010, patients may consult an "on-line" doctor or keep tabs on their physical state and the medications they take with a small computer worn on the wrist like a watch. Some scientists speculate that by the year 2050, most major diseases will have been eliminated, and more people will live to be at least 100 years old.

Whether, or when, human beings reach these goals will depend on the medical technology innovators of tomorrow.

A MEDICAL TIME LINE

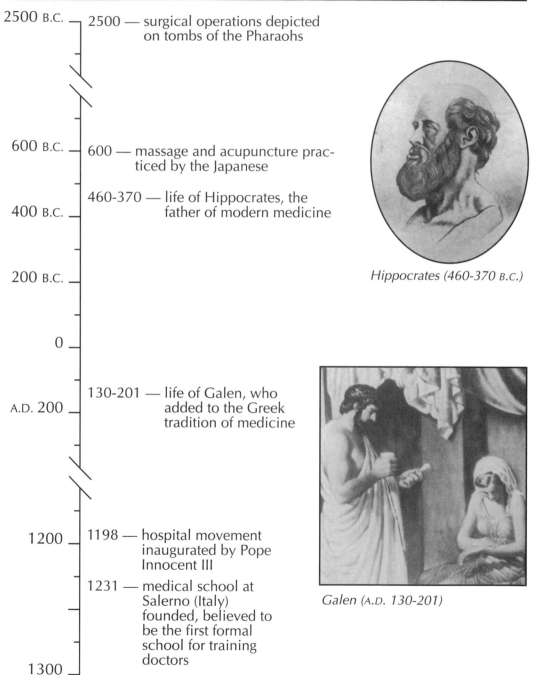

2500 B.C. — 2500 — surgical operations depicted on tombs of the Pharaohs

600 B.C. — 600 — massage and acupuncture practiced by the Japanese

400 B.C. — 460-370 — life of Hippocrates, the father of modern medicine

200 B.C.

0

A.D. 200 — 130-201 — life of Galen, who added to the Greek tradition of medicine

1200 — 1198 — hospital movement inaugurated by Pope Innocent III

1231 — medical school at Salerno (Italy) founded, believed to be the first formal school for training doctors

1300

Hippocrates (460-370 B.C.)

Galen (A.D. 130-201)

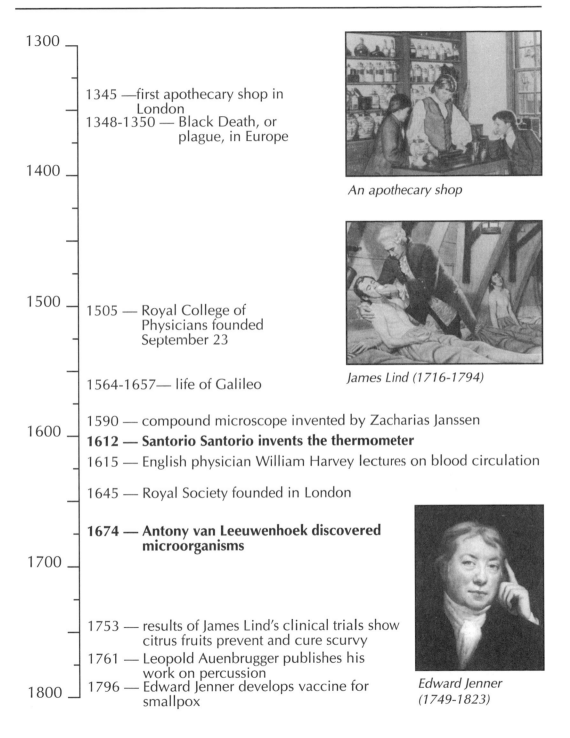

1300

1345 —first apothecary shop in London
1348-1350 — Black Death, or plague, in Europe

1400

An apothecary shop

1500

1505 — Royal College of Physicians founded September 23

1564-1657— life of Galileo

James Lind (1716-1794)

1600

1590 — compound microscope invented by Zacharias Janssen
1612 — Santorio Santorio invents the thermometer
1615 — English physician William Harvey lectures on blood circulation

1645 — Royal Society founded in London

1674 — Antony van Leeuwenhoek discovered microorganisms

1700

1753 — results of James Lind's clinical trials show citrus fruits prevent and cure scurvy
1761 — Leopold Auenbrugger publishes his work on percussion
1796 — Edward Jenner develops vaccine for smallpox

Edward Jenner (1749-1823)

1800

1800

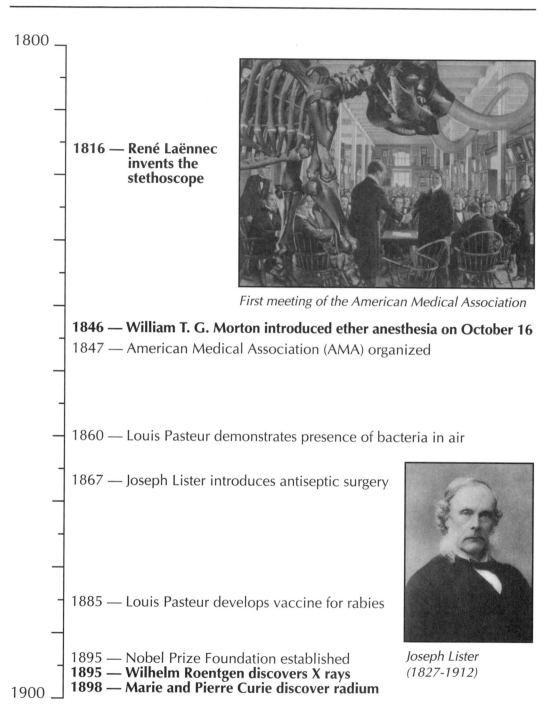

1816 — René Laënnec invents the stethoscope

First meeting of the American Medical Association

1846 — William T. G. Morton introduced ether anesthesia on October 16
1847 — American Medical Association (AMA) organized

1860 — Louis Pasteur demonstrates presence of bacteria in air

1867 — Joseph Lister introduces antiseptic surgery

1885 — Louis Pasteur develops vaccine for rabies

1895 — Nobel Prize Foundation established
1895 — Wilhelm Roentgen discovers X rays
1898 — Marie and Pierre Curie discover radium

Joseph Lister (1827-1912)

1900

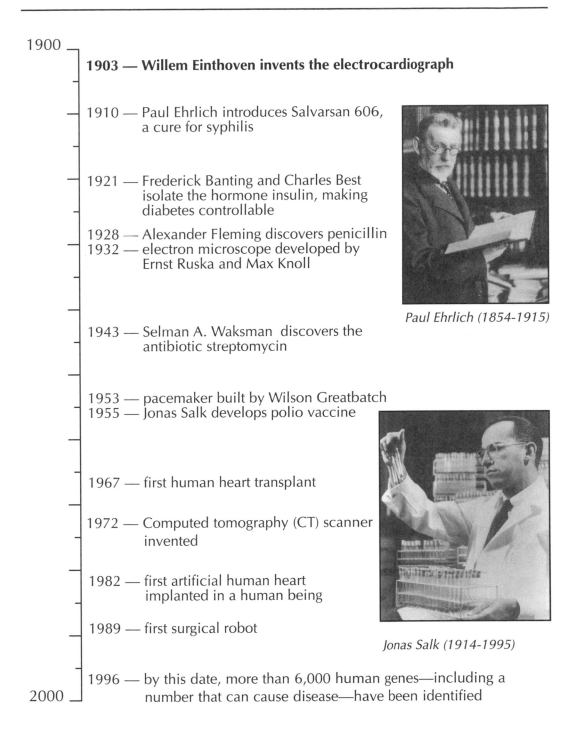

1900

1903 — Willem Einthoven invents the electrocardiograph

1910 — Paul Ehrlich introduces Salvarsan 606, a cure for syphilis

1921 — Frederick Banting and Charles Best isolate the hormone insulin, making diabetes controllable

1928 — Alexander Fleming discovers penicillin
1932 — electron microscope developed by Ernst Ruska and Max Knoll

Paul Ehrlich (1854-1915)

1943 — Selman A. Waksman discovers the antibiotic streptomycin

1953 — pacemaker built by Wilson Greatbatch
1955 — Jonas Salk develops polio vaccine

1967 — first human heart transplant

1972 — Computed tomography (CT) scanner invented

1982 — first artificial human heart implanted in a human being

1989 — first surgical robot

Jonas Salk (1914-1995)

1996 — by this date, more than 6,000 human genes—including a number that can cause disease—have been identified
2000

PERIODIC TABLE OF THE ELEMENTS

KEY

atomic number	8
atomic symbol	O
element name	Oxygen
atomic weight	15.9994

Group Ia	Group IIa	Group IIIb	Group IVb	Group Vb	Group VIb	Group VIIb		Group VIII		Group Ib	Group IIb	Group IIIa	Group IVa	Group Va	Group VIa	Group VIIa	Group VIIIa
1 **H** Hydrogen 1.00794																	2 **He** Helium 4.00260
3 **Li** Lithium 6.941	4 **Be** Beryllium 9.01218											5 **B** Boron 10.81	6 **C** Carbon 12.011	7 **N** Nitrogen 14.0067	8 **O** Oxygen 15.9994	9 **F** Fluorine 18.9984	10 **Ne** Neon 20.179
11 **Na** Sodium 22.9898	12 **Mg** Magnesium 24.305											13 **Al** Aluminum 26.9815	14 **Si** Silicon 28.0855	15 **P** Phosphorus 30.9738	16 **S** Sulfur 32.06	17 **Cl** Chlorine 35.453	18 **Ar** Argon 39.948
19 **K** Potassium 39.0983	20 **Ca** Calcium 40.08	21 **Sc** Scandium 44.9559	22 **Ti** Titanium 47.88	23 **V** Vanadium 50.9415	24 **Cr** Chromium 51.996	25 **Mn** Manganese 54.9380	26 **Fe** Iron 55.847	27 **Co** Cobalt 58.9332	28 **Ni** Nickel 58.69	29 **Cu** Copper 63.546	30 **Zn** Zinc 65.39	31 **Ga** Gallium 69.72	32 **Ge** Germanium 72.59	33 **As** Arsenic 74.9216	34 **Se** Selenium 78.96	35 **Br** Bromine 79.904	36 **Kr** Krypton 83.80
37 **Rb** Rubidium 85.4678	38 **Sr** Strontium 87.62	39 **Y** Yttrium 88.9059	40 **Zr** Zirconium 91.224	41 **Nb** Niobium 92.9064	42 **Mo** Molybdenum 95.94	43 **Tc** Technetium (97)	44 **Ru** Ruthenium 101.07	45 **Rh** Rhodium 102.906	46 **Pd** Palladium 106.42	47 **Ag** Silver 107.868	48 **Cd** Cadmium 112.41	49 **In** Indium 114.82	50 **Sn** Tin 118.71	51 **Sb** Antimony 121.75	52 **Te** Tellurium 127.60	53 **I** Iodine 126.905	54 **Xe** Xenon 131.29
55 **Cs** Cesium 132.905	56 **Ba** Barium 137.33	57-71 Lanthanides	72 **Hf** Hafnium 178.49	73 **Ta** Tantalum 180.948	74 **W** Tungsten 183.85	75 **Re** Rhenium 186.207	76 **Os** Osmium 190.2	77 **Ir** Iridium 192.22	78 **Pt** Platinum 195.08	79 **Au** Gold 196.967	80 **Hg** Mercury 200.59	81 **Tl** Thallium 204.383	82 **Pb** Lead 207.2	83 **Bi** Bismuth 208.980	84 **Po** Polonium (209)	85 **At** Astatine (210)	86 **Rn** Radon (222)
87 **Fr** Francium (223)	88 **Ra** Radium 226.025	89-103 Actinides	104 **Rf** Rutherfordium (261)	105 **Ha** Hahnium (262)	106 **Unh** Unnilhexium (263)	107 **Uns** Nielsbohrium (262)	108 **Hs** Hassium (265)	109 **Mt** Meitnerium (266)									

Lanthanides (Rare Earth Elements)	57 **La** Lanthanum 138.906	58 **Ce** Cerium 140.12	59 **Pr** Praseodymium 140.908	60 **Nd** Neodymium 144.24	61 **Pm** Promethium (145)	62 **Sm** Samarium 150.36	63 **Eu** Europium 151.96	64 **Gd** Gadolinium 157.25	65 **Tb** Terbium 158.925	66 **Dy** Dysprosium 162.50	67 **Ho** Holmium 164.930	68 **Er** Erbium 167.26	69 **Tm** Thulium 168.934	70 **Yb** Ytterbium 173.04	71 **Lu** Lutetium 174.967
Actinides (Radioactive Rare Earth Elements)	89 **Ac** Actinium 227.028	90 **Th** Thorium 232.038	91 **Pa** Protactinium 231.036	92 **U** Uranium 238.029	93 **Np** Neptunium 237.048	94 **Pu** Plutonium (244)	95 **Am** Americium (243)	96 **Cm** Curium (247)	97 **Bk** Berkelium (247)	98 **Cf** Californium (251)	99 **Es** Einsteinium (254)	100 **Fm** Fermium (257)	101 **Md** Mendelevium (256)	102 **No** Nobelium (254)	103 **Lr** Lawrencium (256)

(parentheses indicate mass number of most stable isotope)

anatomy: the structure of a plant or animal, or the study and science of the structure of a plant or animal

anesthesia: the loss of sensation of pain induced by an anesthetic

anesthetic: an agent that causes a lack of sensation with or without loss of consciousness; from the Greek word *anaisthesia,* which means "without feeling." A **local anesthetic,** such as novocaine, affects only a small area of the body.

anode: the electrode through which current passes from the metallic to the nonmetallic conductor; the positively charged electrode

asthma: a respiratory disorder with symptoms of difficult breathing, coughing, and thick mucus production caused by inflammation or spasms of the bronchi

ausculation: the act of listening for sounds made by internal organs during an examination

autopsy: an examination of a body after death has occurred to determine the cause of death, the extent of injuries, or the progress of a disease. Dissection and other methods are used.

bacteria: microorganisms that can cause disease

bronchi: two large channels that lead from the trachea or windpipe to smaller branches and air sacs of the lungs. The singular of bronchi is bronchus, the adjective is bronchial.

cathode: the electrode through which current passes from the nonmetallic to the metallic conductor; the negatively charged electrode

cathode rays: an invisible stream of electrons emitted by the cathode in a vacuum tube

cell: the smallest structural unit of an organism that is capable of independent function. It is made up of an outer membrane, the main mass (cytoplasm), and a nucleus.

chemistry: the study of the composition, structure, properties, and reactions of matter, especially on the atomic or molecular level

computed tomography (CT): a method of examining the body's soft tissues, such as the brain, with a CT scanner. The scanner uses X rays that repeatedly pass through a body part and a computer that calculates tissue absorption at each point scanned, creating a visual picture of the tissue. Formerly called **computed** (or computerized) **axial tomography (CAT).**

concave lens: a round piece of glass that is thicker at the edges than at the center, making light rays diverge, or deflect, in different directions. Objects that these light rays bounce off of appear smaller.

convex lens: a round piece of glass that is thicker at the center than the edges, making light rays converge, or come together. Objects that these light rays bounce off of appear larger.

cure: to restore to health, or a treatment that restores health

disease: a disorder with symptoms that results from infection or another cause

dissect: to separate body tissue by probing or cutting

DNA (deoxyribonucleic acid): a nucleic acid that carries the genetic information in the cell. It consists of two long chains of nucleotides twisted into a double helix and joined by hydrogen bonds. The sequence of bases in nucleotides determines individual hereditary characteristics.

electrocardiogram: the recording made by an electrocardiograph

electrocardiograph: an instrument that makes a record of the electric activity of the heart. Invented by Willem Einthoven in 1903.

electrode: a terminal (usually a wire, rod, or plate) through which an electric current passes between metallic and non-metallic parts of an electric circuit

electromagnet: a piece of soft iron that becomes a magnet when a coil of insulated wire is wrapped around it and an electric current flows through the wire

electromagnetic spectrum: the range and frequency of wave lengths created by radiated energy; that is, the distance between successive wave crests and the number of crests that arrive each second. The waves range from short, high-frequency gamma rays to the long, low-frequency radio waves.

element: in chemistry and physics, a material that cannot be broken down into other substances and which contains only one kind of atom

ether: a highly flammable, colorless liquid derived from the distillation of ethyl alcohol with sulfuric acid. From the Greek word *aither* and the Latin word *aether*, both of which mean "upper air."

experiment: a test under controlled conditions to determine if a theory is probable or whether a treatment is effective

fever: a rise in body temperature, most often caused by an infection or other disease. The normal human temperature is 98.6° Fahrenheit or 37.0° Celsius.

fluorescence: the emission of electromagnetic radiation, especially of visible light, stimulated in a substance by the absorption of radiation

fluoroscope: a device that allows the immediate projection of X-ray images of the body onto a special fluorescent screen. It eliminates the need for taking and developing X-ray photographs but leaves no permanent record.

galvanometer: an instrument used to detect, measure, and determine the direction of small electric currents. Invented about 1825 by Luigi Galvani.

gene: a basic unit of inheritance that occupies a specific place on a chromosome and determines a particular characteristic in an organism

genetics: the study of heredity

magnetic resonance imaging (MRI): a diagnostic technique in which an electromagnetic field stimulates atomic nuclei within a patient's body, causing those nuclei to release energy that is recorded with sensitive receivers. More accurate than X-ray photographs for showing certain body abnormalities.

microorganism: a living thing, such as bacteria, too small for humans to see without a microscope

microscope: an instrument that magnifies objects, some invisible to the human eye. A **light microscope** uses light and either a single lens (simple microscope) or a combination of lenses (compound microscope) to magnify and focus an object. The **electron microscope** uses a beam of electrons to scan and produce an image.

mineral: a natural inorganic (not alive) substance. Rocks are combinations of minerals. A few minerals are elements (i.e., gold, silver, and iron) but most are chemical compounds or mixtures.

Nobel Prize: a highly prestigious international award for achievement in the fields of physics, chemistry, physiology or medicine, literature, economics, and peace

ophthalmology: the study of the eye, its structure, functions, defects, diseases, and treatment

pendulum: an object suspended from a fixed support that, influenced by gravity, swings freely back and forth. Used to regulate devices such as clocks.

percussion: a method of medical diagnosis. The examiner taps a person's chest, back, or abdomen to determine the condition of the body organs in the area, such as the lungs.

phosphorescence: the continuous emission of light, or glow, after exposure to radiation

polonium: a naturally radioactive metallic element, occurring in small quantities in uranium ores, discovered by Marie and Pierre Curie. The chemical symbol is **Po.**

pulse: the rhythmical throbbing of arteries caused by the pumping of the heart. Most easily felt at the wrist or in the neck, the pulse corresponds to each beat of the heart. The average human adult pulse rate is 60 to 80 beats per minute.

pulsilogium: an instrument that measures pulse rate using a pendulum and a scale. Invented by Santorio Santorio in the early 1600s.

radiation: energy transmitted in the form of rays, waves, or particles

radiation therapy: the treatment of certain forms of cancer by radiation given off by special machines. The radiation interferes with the division of the cancer cells and destroys them. Also called **radiotherapy.**

radioactive: emitting radiation spontaneously or by nuclear reaction

radiologist: a doctor who specializes in radiology for diagnoses or treatments

radiology: the branch of medicine that uses X rays and radioactive substances in the diagnosis and treatment of disease

radium: a highly radioactive metallic element found in small amounts in uranium ores, discovered by Marie and Pierre Curie. The chemical symbol is *Ra.*

refraction: the turning or bending of any wave, such as a light wave, when it passes from one medium into another of different density

respiration: the process of breathing. Oxygen is taken from air inhaled by the lungs and carbon dioxide is released from the blood to be exhaled by the lungs.

stethoscope: a medical instrument used for listening to body sounds, such as the heart or lungs. It consists of a bell-shaped piece placed on the patient's skin and connected by plastic or rubber tubes to the examiner's ears. Invented by French physician René Laënnec in 1816.

telescope: an arrangement of lenses and mirrors, or both, that gather light and allow someone looking through the lenses to see distant objects

temperature: the degree of hotness or coldness of a living thing or an environment

thermometer: an instrument that measures the temperature of a human or animal body. Invented in 1612 by Italian physician Santorio Santorio.

tuberculosis: a chronic (long-lasting or frequently occurring) infectious disease that is characterized by the formation of tubercles (swellings or lesions) in the lungs and other tissues of the body

ultrasonography: high-frequency sound waves that bounce off objects, rather than pass through them as normal sound waves do. This bouncing produces echoes, which can be converted into electronic signals that produce an image called a **sonogram.** Doctors use this method to study fetal growth, the heart, and many other organs.

ultrasound: sound waves at frequencies too high for humans to hear

ultraviolet light: the invisible short-wavelength radiation in sunlight that tans and burns the skin

uranium: a radioactive toxic metallic element that easily combines with oxygen and occurs in several minerals. Used in research, nuclear fuels, and nuclear weapons. The chemical symbol is *U.*

virus: a small particle that can reproduce itself within a living cell. It takes over the nucleic acid of the host, reproduces, and then bursts the host cell, releasing new virus particles. Derived from the Latin word for poison, viruses cause many human diseases.

X ray: electromagnetic radiation of short wavelength that can penetrate tissues and record their densities on photographic film. Also the photograph taken with X rays. Discovered by Wilhelm Roentgen in 1895.

BIBLIOGRAPHY

Beier, Lucinda M. *Sufferers and Healers.* London: Routledge, 1987.

Brechar, Ruth and Edgar. *The Rays: A History of Radiology in the United States and Canada.* Baltimore: Williams and Wilkins, 1969.

Burch, George E., and Nicholas P. DePasquale. *A History of Electrocardiography.* Chicago: Year Book Medical Publishers, 1964.

Castiglioni, A. "The Life of Sanctorius." *Medical Life* 38 (1931): 729-85.

Copeman, W. S. C. *Doctors and Disease in Tudor Times.* London: Dawson's, 1960.

Curtis, Robert H. *Great Lives: Medicine.* New York: Scribner's, 1993.

Dobell, Clifford. *Antony van Leeuwenhoek and His "Little Animals."* New York: Harcourt, Brace, 1932.

Duke, Martin. *The Development of Medical Techniques and Treatments: From Leeches to Heart Surgery.* Madison: International Universities Press, 1991.

Ford, Brian J. *Single Lens.* New York: Harper & Row, 1985.

Fox, Daniel M., Marcia Meldrum, and Ira Rezak. *Nobel Laureates in Medicine or Physiology.* New York: Garland, 1990.

Fülöp-Miller, René. *Triumph Over Pain.* Translated by Eden and Cedar Paul. New York: The Literary Guild of America, 1938.

Glasser, Otto. *Wilhelm Conrad Roentgen and the Early History of the Roentgen Rays.* Springfield, Mass.: Thomas Books, 1934.

Grmek, M. D. "Santorio Santorio." *Dictionary of Scientific Biography.* New York: Scribner's, 1971.

Hoogerwerf, S. "Einthoven, Willem." *Dictionary of Scientific Biography.* New York: Scribner's, 1971.

Kervran, Roger. *Laënnec: His Life and Times.* Translated by D. C. Abrahams-Curiel. Oxford: Pergamon Press, 1960.

Knight, Nancy. *Pain and Its Relief.* Washington, D. C.: Smithsonian Institution, 1983.

Levenson, Thomas. *Measure for Measure: A Musical History of Science.* New York: Simon & Schuster, 1994.

McGrew, Roderick E. *Encyclopedia of Medical History.* New York:
McGraw-Hill, 1985.

Major, Ralph D. "Santorio Santorio." *Annals of Medical History*
10 (September 1938): 369-81.

Middleton, W. E. Knowles. *A History of the Thermometer and Its Use in Meteorology.*
Baltimore: The Johns Hopkins University Press, 1966.

Nitske, W. Robert. *The Life of Wilhelm Conrad Roentgen: Discoverer of the
X ray.* Tuscon: The University of Arizona Press, 1971.

Nuland, Sherwin B. *Doctors: The Biography of Medicine.* New York:
Vintage Books, 1988.

Pflaum, Rosalynd. *Grand Obsession: Madame Curie and Her World.*
New York: Doubleday, 1989.

Sigerist, Henry E. *The Great Doctors: A Biographical History of Medicine.* Translated by
Eden Paul and Cedar Paul. New York: Norton, 1933.

Silverman, Mark E. "Willem Einthoven—The Father of Electrocardiography." *Clinical
Cardiology* 15 (1992): 785-87.

Snellen, H.A. *Willem Einthoven (1860-1927): Father of electrocardiography.* Boston:
Kluwer Academic Publishers, 1995.

Talbott, John H. *A Biographical History of Medicine.* New York:
Grune & Stratton, 1970.

Wagner, Henry N. Jr., and Linda E. Ketchum. *Living with Radiation: The Risk, The
Promise.* Baltimore: The Johns Hopkins University Press, 1989.

Webb, Gerald B. *René Théophile Hyacinthe Laënnec.* New York:
Paul B. Hoeber, 1928.

Wiggers, Carl J. "Willem Einthoven (1860-1927): Some Facets of His Life and Work."
Circulation Research 9 (1961): 225-34.

Woodward, Grace S. *The Man Who Conquered Pain.* Boston:
Beacon Press, 1962.

Wyke, Alexandra. "The Future of Medicine." *The Economist* 330, No. 7855
(March 19, 1994): 1-18.

INDEX

eyeglasses, 32, 33, 107

Fahrenheit, Gabriel Daniel, 25
Fahrenheit scale, 25, 26, 27
false teeth, 56-57, 58, 59
farsightedness, 107
feldspar, 57
Ferdinand II, Grand Duke of Tuscany, 25
fever, 15, 27
fluorescent screen, 41, 79-81, 84
fluoroscope, 84, 85
Forane, 71
French Academy of Sciences, 66
French Revolution, 44
Frost, Eben, 64
Frost, Edwin Brant, 84
Frost, G. D., 84

Galen, 17, 18
Galilei, Galileo, 7, 17, 34; invention of thermoscope by, 17, 21, 22
Galvani, Luigi, 109-110, 111
galvanic electricity, 111
galvanized iron, 111
galvanometer, 110, 111, 115; string, 112, 113-114, 115
Garbasso, Antonio, 84
Geissler, Heinrich, 78
genes, cloned, 121
genetic engineering, 121-123
Glasser, Otto, 80
Greatbatch, Wilson, 116
Greek medicine, 8, 12, 17, 18, 19

Green Glass Inn, 75

Harding, Warren G., 102
Harvard Medical School, 55, 59, 61
Hawes, Josiah, 68
Hayden, Granville, 62, 63
heart, human, 43, 48, 49, 50, 105; artificial, 117; controlled by pacemaker, 116-117; electrical activity in, 109, 110, 111, 113, 114, 116; transplant, 117
heartbeats, 105; measurement of, 105, 110-111, 113-115, 116
heart-lung machine, 116-117
Hero of Alexandria, 19, 21
Hinckley, Robert, 65
Hippocrates, 17, 43, 46
Hittorf, Johann, 78
Holmes, Oliver Wendell, 67
Hooke, Robert, 35, 36
hospitals (19th century), 45
humors, theory of, 8-9, 29
Huntington's disease, 121
hydroscope, 23

immune system, 122
induction coil, 78, 79
insensible perspiration, 18-19, 24
insulin, 121

Jackson, Charles, 57, 60, 63; conflict of, with Morton, 66-67, 69, 70-71
Janssen Zacharias, 34
Joliot, Frédéric, 97

40-41; electron, 40-41; operation of, 32-33; simple, 34, 35, 36; uses of, 29, 34, 35, 36-37, 38, 40

Middle Ages, medicine during, 12, 15

midwives, 9, 11

mineral, 96

Molijn, Jacob, 30

Morgagni, Giovanni Battista, 46

Morosini family, 16

Morse, Samuel, 60

Morton, Robert, 56

Morton, William T. G.: conflict of, with Jackson, 66-67, 69, 70; death of, 70; as dentist, 56, 57-58, 59, 62, 64, 68, 70; early years of, 56; experiments of, with ether, 13, 60-61, 62-64, 71; inhaler used by, 63, 64, 65, 66, 69; as medical student, 55, 59-60; patent acquired by, 66, 69

Morton, Willie, 62

Necker, Hôpital, 46, 47

nitrous oxide, 61, 67, 71

Nobel Prize, 86, 89, 97, 100, 101, 116

novocaine, 71

Nuland, Sherwin, 70

ophthalmology, 107-108

opium, 59

pacemaker, 116, 117

Padua, University of, 16, 17, 23, 24, 46

painkillers. *See* anesthetics

Paris, 44-45, 52, 91-92

Pasteur, Louis, 40

pectoriloquy, 50

pendulum, 23

percussion, 47, 48

peritonitis, 46

Peter the Great (Tsar of Russia), 38

pharmacists, 9

phlegm, 8, 29

phlegmatic, 8

photographic plate, 79, 81, 82, 85

physicians (17th century), 9, 10, 11, 12

piezoelectricity, 94

piezo-quartz electrometer, 94

pitchblende, 96, 97, 98

platinum, 81

Plücker, Julius, 78

Poland, 89; controlled by Russia, 89, 90-91

polonium, 97, 101

Polytechnikum, 75

Potterie, Madame de la, 44

Priestley, Joseph, 61

Ptolemy, Claudius, 33

pulse rate, 23

pulsilogium, 23

quartz, 98, 113

radiation, 84, 100, 102; therapy, 100, 101, 103. *See also* radioactivity; radium

ABOUT THE AUTHOR

Robert Mulcahy, born in Brooklyn, New York, in 1971, graduated summa cum laude from the University of Minnesota with a degree in literary studies. Mulcahy now works as an author and an instructional developer of educational computer software. He is also the author of *Diseases: Finding the Cure,* published by The Oliver Press, Inc. Mulcahy lives in St. Paul, Minnesota.

PHOTO ACKNOWLEDGEMENTS

Bettmann Archive: pp. 24, 25, 31, 35, 60, 87, 103.

The Boston Medical Library in the Francis A. Countway Library of Medicine, Boston: pp. 63, 65, 68.

Historical Division, Cleveland Medical Library Association: pp. 22, 39 (bottom), 41, 54, 58, 77, 83, 92, 93, 95, 97.

Library of Congress: pp. 6, 17, 21, 28, 34, 40, 67, 71, 72, 88, 99, 124 (top), 125 (bottom), 126 (bottom).

March of Dimes Birth Defects Foundation: p. 127 (bottom). **Medtronic, Inc.:** pp. 117, 118.

National Library of Medicine: pp. 10, 12, 33, 39 (top), 42, 45, 47, 48, 51, 53, 56, 62, 82, 107, 111, 112, 125 (top), 127 (top).

Otis Historical Archives, National Museum of Health and Medicine, Armed Forces Institute of Pathology: p. 102.

Plants and Flowers, Dover Publications, Inc.: p. 59. **Richard Wacha, Photographer:** p. 27.

U. S. Department of the Interior, National Park Service, Edison National Historic Site: p. 85.

Warner-Lambert Company: pp. 18, 37, 46, 49, 124 (bottom), 125 (middle), 126 (top).

Yale University, Harvey Cushing/John Hay Whitney Medical Library: pp. 14, 20, 104.

The publisher wishes to thank radiologist **David Okrent, M.D.,** Chicago, Illinois, for his careful review of this manuscript.